ARMENIA

Sakina Dhilawala

MARSHALL CAVENDISH
New York • London • Sydney

Reference Edition published 1999 by
Marshall Cavendish Corporation
99 White Plains Road
Tarrytown
New York 10591

© Times Editions Pte Ltd 1997

Originated and designed by
Times Books International, an imprint of
Times Editions Pte Ltd

Printed in Singapore

Library of Congress Cataloging-in-Publication Data:
Dhilawala, Sakina.
    Armenia / Sakina Dhilawala.
      p. cm.—(Cultures Of The World)
    Includes bibliographical references and index.
    Summary: Discusses the geography, history, government,
economy, culture, and religion of the republic atop the
Armenian Plateau in the Caucasus Mountains.
    ISBN 0-7614-0683-2 (library binding)
    1. Armenia (Republic)—Juvenile literature. [1. Armenia
(Republic).] I. Title. II. Series.
DK685.6.D48 1997
945.56—dc21   96–30046
               CIP
               AC

INTRODUCTION

ARMENIANS ARE descendants of a branch of Indo-Europeans. A powerful people in ancient times who had the tenacity to challenge the Roman empire, Armenian history is marked by struggles for independence and domination by foreign powers. Armenia today is home to 3.7 million people, about 96 percent of whom are ethnic Armenians. Minority communities include Russians, Kurds, Yezidis, and Jews.

Today, Armenians are considered the most dynamic of the peoples of the former Soviet Union. They have an outstanding economic growth rate, and standards in education and medical science on par with Western European countries.

Armenians are sociable, hospitable, and faithful to family and community ties. Most Armenians have a pronounced religious belief and are deeply attached to their national church. Armenians are also first-rate farmers and outstanding craftsmen, excelling in handicraft, sculpture, and fine work in precious metals and textiles.

CONTENTS

Two Armenian boys at play.

CONTENTS

A mother treats her child to a pony ride.

GEOGRAPHY

WITH ITS MIGHTY mountains topped with snow, one great lake, and countless ravines and canyons, almost two-thirds of Armenia can be classified as unfit for settled habitation. Large tracts of the Armenian plateau are suitable only to nomads and their herds. Although the country's total land area once equaled that of England and Wales put together, Armenia has never supported a population of more than 5–6 million.

Armenia is situated in southwestern Asia. The country is bordered by Georgia and Azerbaijan to the north and east, Iran and the Azerbaijani province of Nakhichevan to the south, and Turkey to the west. At its greatest extent 2,000 years ago, the area occupied by the Armenian people amounted to well over 100,000 square miles (160,900 square km). Today, Armenian territory covers only about 11,506 square miles (29,800 square km), just slightly larger than the state of Maryland.

Opposite and below: **Armenia is characterized by a mountainous landscape.**

The main Armenian plateau lies at an average height of 4,500–5,500 feet (1,370–1,675 m) above sea level. Armenia is higher than the countries that immediately surround it. Cut off from them on virtually all sides by barriers of lofty hills and mountain peaks, Armenia seems like a massive rock-bound island rising out of the surrounding lowlands, steppes, and plains.

The geological structure of Armenia is unusually interesting, comprising elements from most phases of the earth's history.

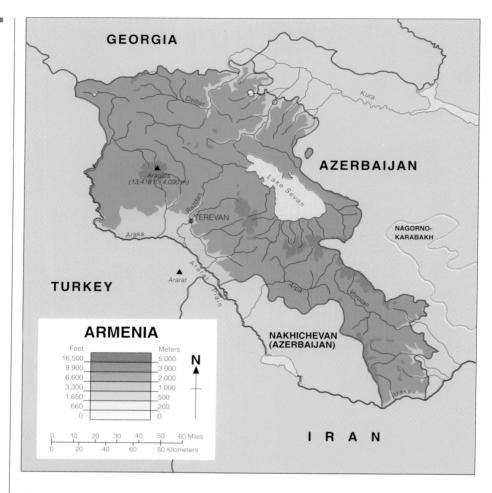

GEOGRAPHIC FEATURES

Armenia's physical features range from heavily forested mountains to elevated plains that are completely bare of trees. The Lesser Caucasus Mountains line the country's northern, eastern, and western borders. The highest point of this range in Armenia is Mt. Aragats (13,418 feet/4,090 m), which is northwest of Armenia's capital, Yerevan.

Armenia is crisscrossed by a number of rivers, and its largest body of water is Lake Sevan, which lies in the northeast.

The Ararat Plain lies in western Armenia, along Armenia's border with Turkey. This is Armenia's breadbowl. Although broken up by valleys and

The Bible states in Genesis 8:4, "... the ark came to rest on the mountains of Ararat." Earthquakes in 1840 destroyed a village, a convent, and a chapel on Mt. Ararat. "Ararat" is the Hebrew form for Urartu, the Assyrian name for a kingdom that existed in the region from the ninth to the seventh century B.C.

deep gorges, this area is a long, narrow strip of land that is heavily cultivated. The Ararat Plain is bisected by the Araks River, Armenia's longest river, which doubles as the country's border with Turkey to the west, and with the Azerbaijani province of Nakhichevan and Iran to the south. The Araks River flows east, joining the Kura River in Azerbaijan and finally emptying into the Caspian Sea.

MT. ARARAT

Today Mt. Ararat is situated in Turkey. However, Armenians once inhabited and ruled the Ararat area, and Mt. Ararat, the legendary resting place of Noah's Ark, holds a special significance for Armenians.

The massif of Mt. Ararat rises on its north and east sides. Out of the massif stand two peaks about seven miles (11 km) apart. Great Ararat is a huge broad-shouldered mass 16,945 feet (5,163 m) high while Little Ararat is an elegant pyramid-like cone 12,877 feet (3,923 m) high.

There is a glacier on the northeast side of Great Ararat. The permanent snow line begins at the unusually high level of 14,000 feet (4,265 m). This is due to the small rainfall and to the upward current of dry air from the plain of the Araks River. Both Great and Little Ararat consist of volcanic rocks.

NOAH'S ARK

In the biblical story of Noah, the ark was a large vessel that saved Noah's family and pairs of all living creatures at the time of the Great Flood. Genesis 6:14-16 describes this floating houseboat. It was made of "gopher" wood, had three decks, and was 450 by 75 by 45 feet (137 by 23 by 14 m) in size. The Sumerian-Babylonian epic of the legendary King Gilgamesh gives a similar but more detailed account of an ark and a flood. Recent attempts to identify the ark's location at Mt. Ararat have been dismissed as pseudoscientific and inconclusive. The most sensational evidence, a large wooden structure found in northeast Turkey, has been dated as only 1,200 years old.

A view of the Arpa River, one of the main tributaries of the Araks River. The Arpa is 80 miles (129 km) long.

ARMENIAN SOIL

Much of Armenia's soil is formed in part from the detritus of volcanic lava, and is rich in nitrogen, potash, phosphates, and other useful chemicals. Typical soils encountered in Armenia are:

• The light brown alluvial earth of the Araks valley and Ararat Plain. The soil in this region is rich in marl (which is a very fertile mix of calcium and clay usually formed in marine environments) but poor in humus (nutrients in the soil formed from decaying vegetable and animal matter), and has been irrigated, fertilized, and cultivated over many centuries.

• The rich brown soil of the drier hill country where Armenians cultivate numerous kinds of crops ranging from corn to valuable plantations of fruit and nut trees.

• The mountain black-earth districts that occupy a large portion of the Armenian uplands. The land here yields excellent crops of the hardier varieties of cereals and vegetables during the brief spring and summer seasons.

• The higher meadow lands covering the slopes of Armenia's great hill and mountain ranges. These rugged highland meadows yield little apart from hay and fodder for flocks and herds but play an important part in the country's economy by providing summer pasture for sheep and cattle.

LAKE SEVAN

Armenia's largest body of water, Lake Sevan, is one of the highest lakes in the world. In the north, Lake Sevan is confined by the long ridge of the Lesser Caucasus Mountains, which cuts off Armenia from Georgia and Azerbaijan, and to the south by the volcanic plateau of Akhmangan, which rises in places to a height of almost 12,000 feet (3,656 m).

The lake itself stands at a level of 6,340 feet (1,932 m). Its waters are sweet and yield delicious salmon trout known as *ishkhan* ("ISH-kahn"), or "prince fish." This lake trout is found only in Lake Sevan. An ancient monastery—the Sevan monastery—stands on a peninsula (until recently, an island) at the northwest corner of the lake. Lake Sevan is fed by many short mountain streams, but has only one outlet—the Razdan River.

Lake Sevan is in danger from many different fronts. Armenians have drawn water from it since 1930, and by the early 1990s its level had dropped almost 20 feet (6 m). Cities and towns dispose of their organic wastes here, polluting its waters. Modern industries also use the lake as a dumping ground.

The Kechut storage lake in central Armenia is an irrigation complex that helps channel water from the Araks River via a 25 mile (40 km) tunnel to Lake Sevan, to raise the water level of the lake. In the late 1980s, the government also built a pipeline to stop waste from entering the lake.

A family makes a temporary shelter in a building damaged by the 1988 earthquake. Prefabricated buildings (picture opposite) from Italy became home for many earthquake victims.

EARTHQUAKES

Earthquakes are a way of life in Armenia as seismic disturbances occur frequently in this geographically active region. Many Armenian lives as well as buildings have been lost in earthquakes. Earthquakes in 1840 destroyed a village, a convent, and a chapel on Great Ararat, the legendary resting place of Noah's Ark.

The most devastating earthquake hit Armenia on the morning of December 7, 1988, killing approximately 25,000 people and causing severe property damage. The force of the earthquake virtually destroyed the towns of Spitak and Gyumri (formerly Leninakan), which lay at its epicenter.

The earthquake cut a wide swathe through Armenia, crippling communications and transportation. Railroads were twisted or blocked and roads were filled with traffic that was backed up for hours, making rescue work difficult. International rescue teams and humanitarian organizations rushed to Armenia's aid.

The December 1988 earthquake is still vivid in Armenians' memory.

THE 1988 EARTHQUAKE

On December 8, 1988, an earthquake that registered between 7.5 and 8.5 on the Richter scale shook Armenia. Its epicenter was 15.5 miles (25 km) southeast of Gyumri. Although Armenia is earthquake-prone, this was the worst earthquake to hit the country in many years.

Medical teams soon arrived in Gyumri. The next day, soldiers also began to arrive in Spitak, one of the worst hit towns, to begin rescue operations. About 1,500 wounded were evacuated by air. Soviet Prime Minister Ryzhkov flew into Yerevan from Moscow on December 8th. Soviet leader Mikhail Gorbachev, who was traveling in the United States, cut short his trip and flew to Armenia.

On December 9, the Armenian government announced that an estimated 700,000 Armenians were directly affected by the earthquake. Four-fifths of Gyumri was destroyed. All 11,000 apartment blocks in the city were damaged or destroyed, leaving thousands homeless. December 10 was declared a national day of mourning throughout the Soviet Union.

Thousands were brought out of the rubble and evacuated. By December 16, the death toll had risen to 23,286. Survivors dragged from the villages totaled 15,300. Altogether 58 villages were destroyed and 1,500 tremors had been reported at the epicenter since the big one struck. The Armenian government estimated that the earthquake caused US$5 billion worth of damage. By December 18, 70,000 people had been evacuated from the earthquake area, and 500,000 people were officially homeless. The final death toll was 24, 817 people. In Gyumri, food rationing was implemented.

The world community also mobilized aid efforts. Forty countries set up disaster funds for earthquake victims. In the days following the earthquake, aid poured into Armenia from all over the world. Businessman Armand Hammer donated $1 million and a plane full of medical equipment. Surgeons arrived with 10 tons (11 tonnes) of medical supplies. Airplanes arrived from Sweden, Syria, Bulgaria, Czechoslovakia, France, and the United States with supplies. Mother Theresa of Calcutta sent nurses to help in the earthquake disaster area. Almost 300 tons (330 tonnes) of food was arriving in Armenia every day. British aid funds totaled $1.3 million, while Soviet firms donated the proceeds of one voluntary working day to the earthquake victims. The son and grandson of then U.S. President George Bush visited Spitak and Yerevan, bringing 40 tons (44 tonnes) of aid with them. The amount of aid that poured into Armenia totaled $17 million.

CLIMATE

Armenia is subjected to cold winters and hot summers, especially in the mountainous and upland areas. The country experiences a wide variety of temperatures, depending on the region. In the winter, temperatures can fall to 40°F below freezing point (–22°C). Armenians living in the north experience between 50 and 60 days of snowfall annually. In certain areas, the snow remains on the ground for up to seven months.

Summers are hot and dry, lasting from July to September. Temperatures range from 79°F (26°C) around Yerevan to 108°F (42°C) elsewhere. Thunderstorms with strong winds but little rain are common, and summer often brings drought. A notable exception to these conditions is the Araks valley, where winters are mild and the summer temperature averages about 90°F (32°F).

Winter near the Geghard Monastery, about 24 miles (38 km) from Yerevan.

Climatically, the most agreeable areas of Armenia are those of the Ararat Plain to the southwest and the wooded mountains and hills in the north, where trees give shade in summer as well as protection from winter gales.

Rainfall occurs throughout the year, but most of Armenia's precipitation occurs in early winter with snow and rain in late spring. Armenia receives an average of 15 inches (38 cm) of precipitation annually.

FLORA

The flora of Armenia is as varied as the climate and landscape. Forests cover only about one-tenth of the country.

Common trees are oak, beech, and hornbeam. Lime, ash, and maple are also plentiful. The woods of Armenia contain the plane tree, yew, walnut, and hawthorn. Small forests of pine and spruce can be found in the northern regions of the country. Birch woods mixed with barberry, wild currant, wild rose, and mountain ash can also be found. Armenia is rich in wild fruits, including grapes, cherry, wild pear, crabapple, damson, medlar, raspberry, and dewberry.

Poppies grow wild in the steppes of Armenia.

The Araks valley favors subtropical plants such as cotton, tobacco, olive, oleander, and mulberry. The peaks are mainly covered with steppe grasses—which are well-suited to dry conditions—and with thorny, shrub-like milk-vetches. Between 4,000 and 6,000 feet (1,200–2,000 m), wild rye and several other grasses flourish. Above 7,000 feet (2,150 m), the ground is often stony and vegetation is sparse.

Bears used to be a common sight in Armenia, but their population has dwindled in recent years due to hunting and the reduction of their habitat.

FAUNA

Armenia has a wide range of animal life: about 10,000 kinds of insects; more than 1,000 invertebrate creatures; and vertebrates include 76 species of mammals, 304 kinds of birds, 44 varieties of reptiles, six sorts of amphibious animals, and 24 species of fish.

The mammals comprise moles and hedgehogs, bats, and various beasts of prey such as leopards, panthers, porcupines, hyenas, polecats, and wildcats. There are also a vast range of domesticated animals ranging from horses to rabbits.

The wolf and the jackal are fairly common and there are also a few bears and badgers. Armenia was once a hunter's paradise, and there are still the occasional wild boar, mountain goat, moufflon, and mottled deer, though these are now rare. Fur-bearing animals include the squirrel, marten, otter, fox, and coypu. In remote districts of the south, wild sheep are found on open uplands.

Among freshwater fish, the most notable are the *ishkhan* (salmon trout) of Lake Sevan. Also found are whitefish, the carp, and the barbel.

Bird life is varied and includes the raven, crow, vulture, hawk, falcon, owl, Caucasian grouse, partridge, quail, snipe, and the rare ular. The pigeon and the dove are common, and there are plenty of waterfowl such as the coot, the teal, and diverse species of duck.

Barbel is a common name for any of several related fish which are so called because of their four fleshy feelers, or barbels, attached to the upper lip and used in the search for food.

NATIVE ANIMALS

COYPU, also known as nutria, is a rodent that has a reddish brown or yellowish brown outer coat, a dark grey undercoat, webbed hind feet, and strong teeth. They grow to a length of 17 to 25 inches (43 to 64 cm) and have long scaly tails. Coypus live in burrows in swampy areas, subsisting chiefly on freshwater plants. The undercoat is processed by furriers to resemble the beaver's pelt.

MARTENS are carnivorous mammals widely distributed throughout the northern hemisphere and valued for their thick fur. They are long and graceful animals with short legs and toes, and are armed with sharp claws. Martens live in hollows of trees when they are not in search of the rodents, birds, and birds' eggs that constitute their food. Martens belong to the family *Mustelidae*, which includes weasels and skunks.

PARTRIDGE is a common name applied to birds of the pheasant family, whose members share plump bodies, short tails, and short beaks adapted for picking up seeds. Their rounded wings and robust breast muscles power their explosive takeoffs to escape predators. They prefer to run, and fly only short distances. Their habitats vary from rocky mountain slopes to forest floors. A few perch in trees. They are native to Armenia and other countries in Europe, Asia, North Africa, and the Middle East. The gray partridge of Europe known to hunters as the Hungarian partridge thrives especially in the grain fields. The chukar, another native species, is pale brownish gray, with bold black and white stripes on the flanks, a white throat bordered in black, and a bright red bill and feet. These birds are about 12 to 14 inches (30 to 36 cm) long.

A fox cub ventures out from its hole. Foxes are indigenous to Armenia.

Yerevan's sports complex, where Armenia's Olympics contenders train for competition.

CITIES

Armenia has a number of well-known cities, both ancient and modern. Yerevan (also known as Erevan), the capital and largest city of Armenia, is on the Razdan River, not very far from Armenia's border with Turkey. In the 1950s, archeologists unearthed a stone slab revealing that the city was founded in 782 B.C. by the Urartian King Argishti I, and that it was named Erebouni. Yerevan's location on the border between the Turkish and Persian empires meant that it was subjected to sieges. Many of Yerevan's old buildings were destroyed when these powers clashed. The city's modern and restored buildings are in traditional Armenian style.

Yerevan is situated in a scenic region noted for its orchards and vineyards, and is an industrial, transportation, communications, and cultural center. It houses a population of about 1.2 million. As Armenia's capital and administrative and governmental center, the city is not part of a province but is one in its own right.

Yerevan is the center of Armenian culture and home to the Yerevan State University (built in 1920), the Armenian Academy of Sciences, a historical museum, a music conservatory, and several technical institutes.

The Matenadaran archives in Yerevan has a rich collection of valuable ancient Armenian manuscripts. Yerevan has several large public libraries, a number of museums and theaters, and botanical and zoological gardens. It is also the site of the ruins of a Roman fortress, a 16th century Turkish fort, and an 18th century mosque.

Another large town with an ancient history is Gyumri. Its name was changed to Alexandrapol in 1837, and to Leninakan in 1924, in honor of Lenin. After the breaking up of the Soviet Union, it was renamed Gyumri. Modern Gyumri is an important industrial town of 150,000 inhabitants. The third largest city in Armenia is Vanadzor (formerly Kirovakan), north of Yerevan.

The middle Araks valley has a number of ancient sites that served successively as the capital of Armenia during different periods of its long history. Chief among these are Armavir, which was important during the Urartian and Hellenistic periods, and Echmiadzin. Echmiadzin, formerly called Vaghar-shapat, is about 12 miles (19 km) from Yerevan. It is the center of the Armenian Apostolic Church. The oldest Armenian domed church, the Cathedral of Echmiadzin, is considered a major monument in Christian architecture.

The predominantly Armenian inhabitants of Stepanakirk—a city in Nagorno-Karabakh—have suffered many hardships due to the ongoing hostilities between Armenia and Azerbaijan for control of the region.

HISTORY

ARMENIAN HISTORY dates back 500,000 years to the Acheulian period, when hunting and gathering peoples crossed the lands in pursuit of migrating herds. For a succession of centuries, Armenia was in constant warfare with invaders—Assyrians, Romans, Byzantines, Arabs, and Turks—all of whom greatly influenced Armenian culture and beliefs.

Ancient Armenia grew out of the Urartu kingdom, a confederation of local tribes formed during the ninth century B.C. It became one of the strongest kingdoms in the near east. The Urartians produced and exported ceramic, stoneware, and metalware, and built fortresses, temples, palaces, and other large public buildings. An Urartian irrigation canal is in use today in Yerevan.

Above: **The remains of a Roman temple in Garni, dating from the first or second century B.C., about 17 miles (27 km) outside Yerevan.**

Opposite: **A *khatchkar* ("KAHCH-kahr") near Lake Sevan. *Khatchkars* are intricately carved memorial stones featuring a cross. Typically Armenian, they go back more than a thousand years.**

The Urartians were invaded many times, first by the Scythians and Cimmerians of the Black Sea region, then by the Persians. From that time, the area that is modern-day Armenia did not see peace for many years. Armenia was part of the Persian empire until Alexander the Great conquered it, bringing the former Persian empire, and with it Armenia, under his control.

Over fifteen hundred years after Alexander's death, Armenia fell into the hands of the Ottoman empire, and remained a part of it until the first quarter of the 20th century. In 1922, Russia made Armenia a Soviet republic. The early 1990s was a time of political and economic reform for the Soviet Union, with many of the Soviet republics making bids for independence. Armenia regained its independence in 1991.

URARTU

The ancient kingdom of Urartu was centered in eastern Turkey. At the height of its prominence in the eighth century B.C., the Urartian kingdom extended as far as present-day northwestern Iran, the Caucasus region (which includes the area between the Black Sea in the west, the Caspian

The helmut of Argishti, who was king of Urartu about 2,750 years ago.

Sea in the east, the Caucasus mountains in the north, and modern-day Iran in the south), and northern Syria. Mt. Ararat, where Noah's Ark is said to have struck land, according to the Old Testament, presumably lay within its borders.

The Urartians were well-known for their skill in craft and for their feats of engineering. They built irrigation canals to water their crops and created sculptures and other ornaments of exquisite craftsmanship.

The Assyrians, who were descendants of the ancient civilization of Mesopotamia centered in the region of the upper Tigris River, regarded Urartu as a threat by the ninth century B.C., although references to Urartu appear in Assyrian records dating approximately 400 years earlier.

The Urartians were also involved in hostilities with the warrior nomads of the Black Sea steppes called the Scythians, and with the Cimmerians, also of the Black Sea region, of whom little is known.

Driven in the late eighth century B.C. from northern Syria, the Urartians subsequently were conquered by the Medes in the early sixth century B.C.

MEDIA

Media, land of the Medes, was an ancient country of western Asia corresponding to the modern provinces of Azerbaijan, Kurdistan, and some of the region of Kermanshah in northwestern Iran.

The Medes were Indo-Europeans, related to the ancient Persians, who entered Iran after 1200 B.C. and came under Assyrian domination. They probably secured their freedom about 625 B.C., when their king, Cyaxares, unified the Median tribes. In 621 B.C., Cyaxares conquered the Persians in southwestern Iran. In the same year, he joined forces with Babylonia in a successful attack on the Assyrians that led to the eventual destruction of the Assyrian empire. At its height, the Medes kingdom included western Iran, northern Mesopotamia, and part of Anatolia.

After the Medes were overthrown in 550 B.C. by the Persian conqueror, Cyrus the Great, Media was a province in successive empires of the region.

PERSIAN AND GREEK RULE

In the sixth century B.C., the Urartu kingdom, after a brief rule under the Medes, fell to the Persians under Cyrus the Great. Persia ruled Armenia from the sixth to the fourth century B.C. During this period, Armenia was one of the satrapies (provinces) of the Persian empire, governed by satraps (viceroys) of

The Armenian government has begun a program to restore ancient sites in Yerevan, like this courtyard from the Urartu period.

Armenia's royal Orontid family. Much of Persian culture and religion was absorbed by the Armenians during this period.

In the fourth century, Persia was conquered by Alexander the Great of Macedonia. Under its new ruler, Armenian culture absorbed Greek influences. This was a period of great economic success. Armenian cities thrived due to their position at the crossroads of trade routes connecting the Mediterranean with China, India, and Central Asia.

After Alexander's death in 323 B.C., his generals split his empire into three kingdoms. Hellenistic rule over Armenia finally came to an end in the second century B.C. when a local general, Artaxias, declared himself king of Greater Armenia (the region of northern Armenia) and founded a new dynasty in 189 B.C. Artaxias expanded his territory by defining the borders of his land and unifying the Armenians.

The Armenian kingdom reached its peak during the reign of Tigran the Great (95–55 B.C.). Under Tigran, Armenian territory stretched from the Caspian Sea to the Mediterranean, and from the Caucasus (which included parts of modern Georgia and Azerbaijan) to Palestine. This brought the Armenians into conflict with the Roman empire, and Tigran was forced into an alliance with Rome. Armenia became the focus of Roman and Parthian-Persian rivalry for the next four hundred years.

Armenia was the first nation to adopt Christianity as the state religion, in A.D. 301. In the later part of the fourth century, much of Armenia was divided between Byzantine and Persian rulers. The Persians continued to fight for remaining Armenian lands until the Arabs invaded in the seventh century.

Tigran the Great (reigned 95–55 B.C.) brought the Armenian kingdom to its zenith, expanding its territory as far south as Palestine and as far east as the Caspian Sea.

ALEXANDER THE GREAT

Alexander the Great (356–323 B.C.) was born in Pella, the capital of Macedonia. His father was King Philip II of Macedonia and his mother Princess Olympias of Epirus. As a child Alexander was taught the princely art of warfare as well as educated in philosophy, mathematics, and science. The Greek philosopher Aristotle was one of the prince's tutors. In 336 B.C., Philip was assassinated. Alexander succeeded him and executed his father's alleged murderers along with those who opposed him. No stranger to war—at age 16, he led an army in battle—Alexander's Persian expedition to replenish his war-depleted wealth began in 334 B.C. With 30,000 infantry and 5,000 cavalry composed of Macedonians and Greeks,  he crossed the Dardanelles. At the river Granicus (modern Kocabas), near Troy, he defeated an army of Persian and Greek mercenaries. The states of Asia Minor soon submitted to him.

Alexander continued his journey southward toward Syria. In 333 B.C., at Issus in northeastern Syria, he defeated the great Persian army of King Darius III. Darius fled, abandoning his army and his family. Alexander met Darius again two years later, while crossing Mesopotamia to reach the Tigris River. In a battle on the plain of Gaugamela, Alexander again emerged victorious, although, once again, Darius retreated, this time to Bactria. When Darius was killed by the satrap of Bactria in 330 B.C., Alexander achieved his ambition to become the ruler of the Persian empire.

In 332 B.C., Alexander founded the city of Alexandria in Egypt. The city later became the literary, scientific, and commercial center of the Greek world. By 332 B.C., Alexander's domain stretched along and beyond the southern shores of the Caspian Sea, including modern Afghanistan, and northward toward modern Turkmenistan.

Still not satisfied with his conquests, Alexander crossed the Indus River into Punjab in 326 B.C. His army, however, refused to proceed further with him. Instead they sailed to the Persian Gulf and crossed the desert to Media. Insufficient food and water took its toll on the men. The tireless Alexander gathered information on the Persian Gulf in preparation for even more conquests, but in 323 B.C., not long after his arrival in Babylon, he became ill and died.

Alexander, one of history's military geniuses, was a brilliant strategist. His speed in traversing and conquering vast expanses of territory is unparalleled. He brought surveyors, engineers, scientists, and historians on his campaigns, and left relatives and close friends entrenched in conquered domains before proceeding onward to his next goal. Alexander founded and named several cities Alexandria after himself. Many Greeks from his army settled in these cities, and Greek influence grew as the use of their language and culture spread.

THE ADOPTION OF CHRISTIANITY

Christianity was introduced to Armenia by the apostles Thaddeus and Bartholomew in the first century A.D. In A.D. 301, Armenia embraced Christianity as the state religion, thus being the first nation to do so. The then ruler, King Tiridates III, was converted by Grigor Partev (Gregory the Parthian), named by the Armenians "The Illuminator" because he enlightened the ruler and the nation.

The Persian empire's attempts to impose Zoroastrianism on the Christian Armenians met with great resistance. In A.D. 451, under the leadership of Vardan Mamikonian (a statue of whom graces Yerevan), Armenians faced the Persians in the Battle of Avarayr. Although they were defeated, being heavily outnumbered, guerrilla warfare continued in the mountainous regions. Finally, under Vahan Mamikonian, Vardan's nephew, the Persians came to terms with the Armenians and freedom of worship was restored with the Treaty of Nvarsag (A.D. 484).

THE ARAB AND SELJUK INVASIONS

Armenians lived under Arab control for 300 years from the seventh century A.D. Many Armenians fled to Byzantine-controlled western Armenia to avoid conversion to Islam, the religion brought by the Arab conquerors.

The period under Arab rule saw a revival in Armenian art, documentation, trade, and church and secular literature. History was documented by Moses of Khoren, John of Drashanakert, and Thomas Arzruin. The poetry and hymns of Gregory of Narek were also recorded during this period, and many of them are still used in churches today.

In A.D. 1071, Armenian land fell under the rule of the Seljuk Turks, nomadic warriors from Central Asia, when the Turks defeated the Byzantines in the Battle of Manzikert. This invasion forced a number of Armenians to move south toward the Taurus mountains close to the Mediterranean Sea. In 1080, under the leadership of Ruben, these Armenians founded the kingdom of Cilicia or Lesser Armenia, which comprised the region of the plateau surrounding the central Taurus mountains and the plain between the Taurus and Armanus mountains.

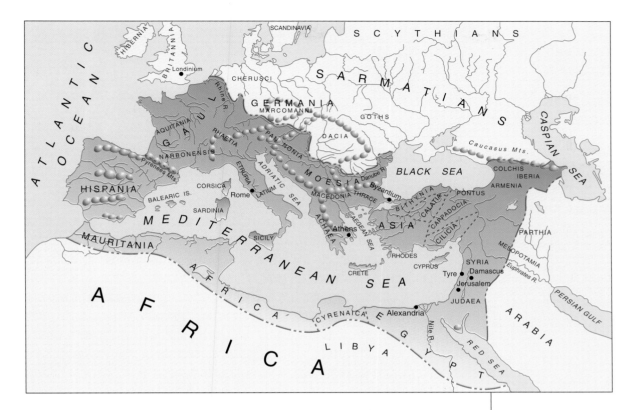

THE GOLDEN AGE OF ARMENIAN ILLUMINATION

The Cilician period is regarded as the "Golden Age of Armenian Illumination" as it enjoyed high culture and great prosperity at a time when the Armenian homeland was slowly falling into ruin.

Close contact with the Crusaders and with Europe led the Cilicians to adopt Western European ideas, including its feudal structure of barons, knights, and serfs. The Cilicians even adopted the lavish decorations and contemporary paintings of the Europeans. Latin influence was strong in Cilicia due mainly to the great military expeditions of Emperor Frederick II (1194–1250) and King Louis IX (1214–1270). Many Italian colonies were also established in Cilicia and Armenian colonies founded in Italy.

In the late 16th century, the Armenians fell under the control of the Ottoman empire, a Muslim Turkish empire descended from the Seljuks. A small part of Armenia came under Persian rule.

Armenia's position on the trade route between the Mediterranean and Asia made it an attractive target for empire builders. This map of the Roman empire shows Cilicia southwest of Armenia.

Opposite (top): **Ottoman Sultan Abdul Hamid II. (Bottom): The Sardapat War Memorial commemorates Armenia's 1918 battle with the Turkish army.**

Below: **An engraving of Abbas I of Persia. Many Armenians escaped the conflict between the Ottoman empire and Persia by migrating eastward to countries in Asia.**

OTTOMAN RULE

Under Ottoman rule, Armenians lost all vestiges of an independent political life. The Ottoman rulers advocated a policy of moving populations of Armenian regions to the Ottoman capital, pulling in the resources of skilled artisans and the merchant class.

Shah Abbas of Persia also figured prominently in the exodus of Armenians in the early 17th century. The Shah, who had made peace with the Ottoman empire in 1590, advanced in 1603 to retake Azerbaijan from the Turks. In the process, he removed some 300,000 Armenians to the south. In 1605, he resettled Armenian merchants and artisans from Julfa in his new capital, Isfahan.

During the last quarter of the 19th century, Ottoman Armenians agitated for change against discrimination, heavy taxation, and armed attacks. The use of terrorism to relay their message did not go down well with the Ottomans who saw this as a means to dissect their empire. Some 200,000 Armenians were massacred between 1894 and 1896.

During World War I (1914–1918), the Turks began killing or driving away the entire Armenian population. The Ottoman government wanted to make room for Turkish and Kurdish settlers, and moreover believed that the Armenians were pro-Russian. Approximately one and a half million Armenians died during this ethnic cleansing.

At the end of World War I, after the rise of the Bolsheviks in Russia, an independent Republic of Armenia was declared in Russian Armenia in May 1918. However, external forces, especially pressure from the Turks, led to the collapse of the republic in 1920. The Soviet Red Army moved into the territory, and in 1922 Armenia was made a Soviet republic.

THE ARMENIAN GENOCIDE

A bleak period in Armenian history stretches from the late 19th century to the early 20th century. This period was marked by the death of one and a half million Armenians, who were killed by the Turks in 1915–1916.

In the late 19th century, following the example of Europe, the Ottoman sultans decided to bring about progressive change to the empire under the banner of the *Tanzimat* ("TAHN-zee-MAHT," meaning "reorganization"). Planned and begun under Mahmud II, the Tanzimat modernized the Ottoman empire by extending the reach of government into all aspects of life, overshadowing the autonomous guilds that had monopolized most governmental functions prior to this. A modern administration and army were created along Western lines, with highly centralized bureaucracies. A secular system of education and justice were organized. Large-scale public works programs modernized the

infrastructure of the empire, building new cities, roads, railroads, and telegraph lines. New agricultural methods also contributed to the Ottoman revitalization.

Taking advantage of this, Armenians in the eastern provinces of the Ottoman empire began to promote the notion of an independent Armenian nation.

All reform movements were brought to an end during the reign of Sultan Abdul Hamid II (1876–1909) and especially after the Russo-Turkish War of 1877–1878, which signaled the decline of the Ottoman empire in the Balkans and the Caucasus. The Turks blamed the Armenians, who were thought to be pro-Russian. This resulted in a series of massacres from 1894 to 1896.

Turkish persecution of the Armenians continued during World War I when they were killed or forced to relocate. Many died from heat and exhaustion during their arduous march through the Syrian, Mesopotamian, and Arabian deserts.

A SOVIET REPUBLIC

An old steam train with the Soviet insignia, a reminder that Armenia used to be a Soviet republic.

Armenia, Azerbaijan, and Georgia signed a treaty to form the Transcaucasian Soviet Federated Socialist Republic in March 1922. Despite promises by the Soviet Union to grant Armenia control of Nagorno-Karabakh and Nakhichevan where a large population of Armenians resided, the two regions were placed under Azerbaijani governance in 1923. In 1936, the Transcaucasian Federation was abolished and Armenia as well as Azerbaijan and Georgia became separate constituent republics of the Soviet Union.

The first priority of the Soviet regime was to neutralize nationalist forces in Armenia. This it accomplished by banning the political group, the Dashnaks, in November 1923. The Dashnaks were politically active in seeking an independent Armenia. In addition, persecution of the Church began in the 1920s as places of worship and religious presses were also closed. The "Russification" of Armenia not only saw that age-old rural beliefs were no longer practised, but it also led to the destruction of Armenian literature and culture. The works of many prominent Armenian writers, such as Raffi (Akop Melik-Akopian), were destroyed or banned during this period.

The breakup of the Soviet Union beginning in the 1980s led to Armenia's second attempt at gaining independence. In 1990, the Armenian National Movement won a majority of seats in parliament and formed a government. On September 21, 1991, the Armenian people overwhelmingly voted in favor of independence in a national referendum and an independent Armenia came into being.

THE STRUGGLE FOR NAGORNO-KARABAKH

Nagorno-Karabakh was at one time a state in its own right. About 80 percent of its population of approximately 180,000 are Armenians. In 1921, the Caucasian section of the Russian Communist Party declared the country part of Armenia. This decision was reversed a few days later by the commissioner for nationalities, Joseph Stalin, who placed it under Azerbaijani control.

The pressure to unify Nagorno-Karabakh with Armenia started in 1988 with a demonstration in Yerevan and elsewhere against Azerbaijani repression of the Armenians in Nagorno-Karabakh. This resulted in a series of killings of Armenians in Azerbaijan. Moscow intervened by imposing direct rule over Nagorno-Karabakh. The protests continued.

Russia returned control of Nagorno-Karabach to Azerbaijan in November 1989. Armenia protested and declared Nagorno-Karabakh part of the Armenian republic. After renewed ethnic violence in Azerbaijan, Soviet troops stormed in and a state of emergency was established that lasted until August 1991.

Azerbaijan and Armenia became independent in 1991. After the last Russian troops left Nagorno-Karabakh in early 1992, the conflict turned into a full-scale war. By the end of 1993, Armenian forces had expelled Azerbaijani forces from Nagorno-Karabakh and occupied a considerable part of Azerbaijani territory. International efforts were pulled in to help bring an end to the war. Despite the efforts of the Organization for Security and Cooperation in Europe, Iran, Turkey, and the United States to mediate in the conflict, the war still continues.

The battle over Nagorno-Karabakh has taken the lives of more than 16,000 people, and over a million people, Armenian and Azerbaijani, have been displaced.

A woman weeps over the grave of her son, a casualty of the conflict over Nagorno-Karabakh, as her husband serenades him.

GOVERNMENT

ARMENIA REMAINED A PART of the Ottoman empire for 400 years—from the early 16th century to the early 20th century. Towards the latter part of the 19th century, human rights violations against the Christian Armenians by the Turkish authorities intensified Armenian nationalist sentiment, which was already aroused by nationalist literature. Nationalist parties—the Dashnaks and the Hnchaks—worked to bring the Armenian question on the international agenda. European authorities expressed concern about the Armenian situation, but did little when thousands of Armenians were massacred between 1894 and 1896.

During World War I, the Turkish authorities, considering the Christian Armenians sympathetic to their Russian foes, embarked on a program of forced deportations and massacres. This resulted in the death of nearly one and a half million Armenians, and has been called the "first genocide of modern times." Thousands of Armenians migrated to Russian Armenia.

The Russians were galvanized into taking action. In 1918, an independent Republic of Armenia was formed under the Dashnaks. For two years, the Dashnak administration struggled with the republic's economic problems, while fending off attacks from the Turks and fighting for international recognition. In December 1920, the Dashnaks turned over the administration to the Communists, forming the Soviet Republic of Armenia.

Armenia declared its independence on August 23, 1990. After a year of opposition from the government in Moscow, Armenia withdrew from the Soviet Union in September 1991. Since then, much of the government's work has been focused on Armenia's dispute with Azerbaijan over Nagorno-Karabakh.

Opposite: **An eagle symbolizes the might and heroism of Armenians. The eagle, a symbol of the people who populated Armenia before the creation of Urartu, is a popular motif in Armenia.**

Below: **The federal building in Yerevan houses government ministries.**

A mass meeting of the opposition in Yerevan, in 1996.

THE POLITICAL SYSTEM

Armenia is a republic with a presidential governing system. Its official name is Hayastani Hanrape-tut'yun. From 1990 to 1995, the political, legal, social, and economic relationships of the previous political system were slowly dismantled.

The political life of the country changed on July 5, 1995, when Armenians voted to adopt the constitution of the Republic of Armenia. The constitution provides legal guarantees of civil rights, the development of democratic institutions, and the creation of a market economy to secure the future stability of the state.

The president oversees the normal activity of the executive, legislative, and judicial authorities. The same person cannot hold the office of president for more than two consecutive terms.

LEVON TER-PETROSSIAN, PRESIDENT OF ARMENIA

Levon Ter-Petrossian was born in 1945 in Aleppo, Syria. His family repatriated to Armenia in 1946. Graduating from Yerevan State University in 1968, he continued his studies at the Leningrad Institute of Oriental Studies until 1972, specializing in Armenian and Assyrian philology. From 1972 to 1978, he was a researcher at the Institute of Literature in the Armenian Academy of Sciences. From 1978 to 1985, he was the academic secretary of the Matenadaran (Institute of Ancient Manuscripts).

Ter-Petrossian's political career started in the 1960s with his participation in Armenia's many student movements. In 1988, he became the leader of the committee formed to plan ways to reclaim Nagorno-Karabakh. From December 10, 1988 to May 31, 1989, he and other members of the committee were under arrest in Moscow. In August 1989 he was elected deputy of Armenia's Supreme Soviet. Later that year he joined the Armenian National Movement, a group he would eventually lead.

On October 16, 1991, Ter-Petrossian was elected as Armenia's first president. He was re-elected in 1996 with 53 percent of the vote.

In 1987, Levon Ter-Petrossian received a Ph.D. in philological sciences. Ter-Petrossian, who has written numerous papers and articles on Armenian-Assyrian cultural ties and the Armenian Cilician State, is a member of the Writer's Union of Armenia and the French-Asian Society.

ARMENIA'S DECLARATION OF INDEPENDENCE

The rights of the citizens of the Republic of Armenia are encompassed in its Declaration of Independence. There are 12 points in the Declaration:

1. The Armenian Soviet Socialist Republic is renamed the Republic of Armenia and has its own flag, coat of arms, and anthem.

2. The Republic of Armenia is a self-governing state, with the power to act independently of other states. Only the constitution and laws of the Republic of Armenia are valid for the whole territory.

3. The people of the Republic exercise the authority of their state directly and through representative bodies on the basis of the constitution and laws of the Republic. The Supreme Council speaks on their behalf.

4. Residents of Armenia are granted citizenship of Armenia. Armenians of the Diaspora also have the right of this citizenship. Armenia guarantees the free and equal development of its citizens regardless of national origin, race, or creed.

5. To guarantee the security of the country and the inviolability of its borders, the Republic creates its own armed forces, internal troops, and organs of state and public security. Armenia has its share of the Soviet Union's military apparatus but determines the regulation of military service for its citizens independently. Military units and military bases or buildings of other countries can be located in Armenia only if permitted by Armenia's Supreme Council. The armed forces of the Republic of Armenia can be deployed only by a decision of its Supreme Council.

Armenians are guaranteed freedom of speech and demonstration. Here, they march to protest the blockade of Armenia by Azerbaijan, which has caused food shortages.

6. Armenia conducts an independent foreign policy. It establishes direct relations with other states and national-state units of the former Soviet Union, and participates in the activity of international organizations.

7. The national wealth of the Republic of Armenia—the land, the earth's crust, airspace, water, and other natural resources, as well as economic, intellectual, and cultural capabilities—are the property of its people. Their regulation, usage, and possession are determined by the laws of the Republic. The Republic has the right to its share of the national wealth of the Soviet Union.

8. The Republic of Armenia determines the principles and regulations of its economic system. It creates its own money, national bank, and financial and tax systems based on multiple forms of property ownership.

Armenia's coat of arms features an eagle and a lion holding a shield. Mt. Ararat—with Noah's Ark on it—lies in the heart of the shield, surrounded by a double-headed eagle, scepter-bearing lions, and two doves. Below the shield are the hilt of a sword, a stylized branch, a sheaf of wheat, and the links of a broken chain.

9. On its territory, the Republic of Armenia guarantees freedom of speech, press, and conscience; separation of legislative, executive, and judicial powers; a multiparty system; equality of political parties under the law; depolitization of law enforcement bodies and armed forces.

10. Armenian is the state language in all spheres of the Republic's life. The Republic creates its own system of education and of scientific and cultural development.

11. The Republic of Armenia wants to achieve international recognition of the 1915 genocide in Ottoman Turkey and Western Armenia.

12. Until the new constitution is approved, this Declaration is the basis for the introduction of amendments to the current constitution.

Prime Minister Hrant Bagratian.

GOVERNMENT LEADERS

The government is headed by the president who appoints a prime minister to oversee the duties of the executive branch. The prime minister, in turn, is responsible for recommending members of the government, who are then officially appointed by the president.

THE NATIONAL ASSEMBLY

Legislative powers are exercised by the National Assembly, formerly known as the Armenian parliament. Its president, currently Babken Ararktsian, is elected by its members.

HRANOUSH HAGOBIAN

Armenia's National Assembly, which was elected in 1995, has 12 women legislators, a large increase from the previous assembly. One of them is Hranoush Hagobian. A former member of the Communist Party, Hagobian switched allegiance long ago and is now an outspoken supporter of President Levon Ter-Petrossian.

Hagobian, a university graduate with degrees in mathematics, law, and political science, does not apologize for her Communist Party past, where she spent years as First Secretary of the Armenian Communist Youth Movement. She strenuously rejects the label of politician, calling herself instead an Armenian nationalist. Appointed head of the Social Affairs, Health, and Ecology Committee, Hagobian has been hard at work laying the groundwork for improving the quality of life for her fellow Armenians. Hagobian has no illusions about what needs to be done; she admits that the country needs reforms in all three sectors, and she has made this one of her priorities. She also led the Armenian delegation to the Fourth United Nations World Conference on Women held in Beijing in 1995.

The election laws adopted in 1995 set the number of deputies at 190. Assembly elections were held on July 5, 1995, filling the 190 seats for a four-year period. At the next elections, the size of the Assembly will be reduced to 131 members.

The National Assembly is a single-chamber representative body which convenes twice a year—in the spring (from early February to late June) and fall (from late September to late December). Extraordinary sessions, however, may be convened at the discretion of the presidium of the National Assembly (a committee that acts on behalf of the National Assembly when it is in recess), by a third of the deputies, the president of the National Assembly, or the president of the republic.

Lenin and a Russian slogan dominated the assembly of the Armenian Soviet Socialist Republic. The right to withdraw from the Soviet Union was written into the constitution of each republic, but until 1991, this was found to be a right that could not be practiced.

THE JUDICIAL BRANCH

Armenia's civil justice system is still administered through two types of courts—the district courts and the Supreme Court. Two new courts, the military court (tribunal) and the military chamber of the Supreme Court, were established in August 1992 to handle specific cases involving military personnel.

Regulation of the military court was subsequently approved by the National Assembly. However, the military court has yet to be formed and cases assigned to its jurisdiction are currently still tried by the district courts. The military chamber of the Supreme Court is already hearing specific cases, although it does not yet have its full complement of judges.

A traffic police officer issuing a ticket to a motorist. To appeal the ticket, the motorist would have to take the case to district court.

Armenia's district courts have no specialized judicial divisions. Each court is made up of a senior judge, several judges, and elective lay associates. Armenia's district courts have jurisdiction over both criminal and civil cases. In certain cases administered by law, district judges take on administrative cases as well.

The Supreme Court is headed by the chief justice. Each other justice is assigned to one of the following three chambers—criminal, civil, or military. The Supreme Court also has elective lay associates. The criminal, civil, and military chambers make up the lower level of the Supreme Court's structure.

The full-member Supreme Court sitting and presided over by the chief justice is called a "plenum." The plenum, including the chief justice, consists of 33 members.

In addition to this, a constitutional court was created in 1995.

CONSTITUTIONAL COURT

In addition to the existing judicial system, a need was felt for a court that would pronounce judgment on issues of adherence to the constitution. This was brought to the attention of the National Assembly, and assembly members approved the idea.

On December 6, 1995, a constitutional court consisting of nine members (five appointed by the National Assembly and four by the president) was created.

The constitutional court is responsible for ruling on matters such as whether laws, presidential decrees, and government resolutions that are passed by legislators are constitutional. The court also judges the constitutionality of international agreements in which Armenia is involved or is considering involvement, and resolves disputes concerning election results and referenda.

The Commonwealth of Independent States, or CIS, is an association of former Soviet republics. It was established on December 8, 1991. Members include Armenia, Georgia, Russia, Ukraine, Belarus, Kyrgistan, Tajikistan, Turkmenistan, Uzbekistan, Azerbaijan, and Moldova. CIS members cooperate in economic and defense matters.

DEFENSE

Following the breakup of the Soviet Union in 1991, Armenia became a member of the Commonwealth of Independent States (CIS). Armenia participates in the CIS collective security system, but it has also established its own armed forces, now estimated to be 33,000 strong. There is, in addition, a paramilitary force attached to the Ministry of Internal Affairs.

In 1992, an estimated 2.3 percent of budgetary expenditure was allocated to defense. Armenia joined the North Atlantic Treaty Organization's (NATO) "partnership for peace" program of military cooperation in 1994.

FOREIGN RELATIONS

Since 1991, the Armenian government has moved quickly and effectively to establish friendly and close diplomatic and economic ties with the outside world. More than 120 countries have formally recognized Armenia, and over 70 have officially established diplomatic relations.

Eleven countries have opened embassies and missions in Armenia: the United States, Russia, China, Egypt, France, Georgia, Germany, Greece, Iran, Canada, and the United Kingdom. On its part, Armenia has secured a permanent presence in several countries, opening embassies and missions in Argentina, Austria, Belgium, Bulgaria, Canada, Croatia, Cyprus, Georgia, Germany, Greece, Egypt, France, The Vatican, Hungary, Iran, Italy, Luxembourg, Kazakhstan, Kyrgistan, Lebanon, Moldova, Morocco, Netherlands, Romania, Russia, Slovenia, Syria, and the United Kingdom.

Armenia has also become an active participant in global issues and concerns. It is a member of prominent international organizations, including the United Nations, the World Bank, the International Monetary Fund, the World Health Organization, the European Bank for Reconstruction and Development; regional security bodies such as the Conference on Security and Cooperation in Europe and Interpol; humanitarian organizations such as UNIDO, UNESCO, and the United Nations Development Program; and other global bodies such as the International Telecommunications Organization and the Customs Cooperation Council. Since Armenia's independence in 1991, the United States and Armenia have strengthened their relations.

A significant event in U.S.-Armenian relations was the meeting between U.S. President Bill Clinton and President Levon Ter-Petrossian. The August 9, 1994 meeting in the Oval Office between the two heads of state marked the beginning of a new chapter in U.S.-Armenian relations, one that both believe will help to bring lasting peace and prosperity to Armenia as well as to the entire Caucasus region.

Opposite: **Armenian troops participating in a joint CIS defense exercise.**

Below: **Making sure all is in place for the guard of honor for a visiting head of state.**

ECONOMY

UNDER THE SOVIET CENTRAL PLANNING SYSTEM, Armenia's economy developed into a modern industrial sector supplying machine building equipment, textiles, and other manufactured goods. However, since the conflict over Nagorno-Karabakh, the country's economy has been hit severely. Azerbaijan and Turkey have blockaded pipeline and railroad traffic to Armenia, leaving the country with chronic energy shortages. Apart from that, there is also a shortage of bread and other goods.

Despite the setbacks, a radical reform program implemented in 1994 helped to boost the country's economy. One of these reforms is the privatization of large and medium-sized enterprises. Although Armenia has pursued swifter progress in privatization than its neighbors, it has not been able to meet targets due largely to resistance from ministries and the lack of technical resources.

Left: **A shepherd tending his sheep.**

Opposite: **A street market in "Little Bangladesh," the poorest area of Yerevan, with a myriad wares for sale.**

EMPLOYMENT

The employed workforce in Armenia is approximately 1.9 million people. Currently, nearly half of Armenia's workforce is employed by the state. However, as the government's privatization program takes off, there will

be a larger shift in the workforce from the government to the private sector. In the private sector, the agricultural industry employs up to 30 percent of the workforce.

Armenia's unemployment figure has been rising steadily since 1992. Tackling the unemployment problem is one of the biggest challenges faced by the Ter-Petrossian administration. The official unemployment figure for 1995 was 7.4 percent but economists believe the actual figure is a lot higher. Many unemployed Armenians do not bother to register for state-provided unemployment benefits, which people claim is so low it is not sufficient to cover their transportation cost to and from the unemployment office.

Armenia's escalating unemployment is exacerbated by the Azerbaijani economic blockade. Those who have jobs count their blessings.

Year	Registered Number Unemployed	% of Total Population
1992	56,000	3
1993	87,000	4
1994	91,000	4

AGRICULTURE

Agriculture is the second largest sector of the Armenian economy. It is also the second largest employer in Armenia, employing about 30 percent of the workforce. In the agricultural areas, which include the fertile Araks valley, Armenians grow vegetables, fruit (especially grapes), tobacco, and sugar beet, among other crops. Agricultural products include specialty teas and oils such as geranium, rose, and peppermint.

As local food production does not satisfy domestic needs, Armenia imports large quantities of food from abroad. During the Soviet period, Armenia imported almost two-thirds of its bread and dairy products from other Soviet republics. The economic blockade by Azerbaijan and the civil war in Georgia caused food supplies to diminish. In the early 1990s, however, in contrast to industrial production, agricultural output increased considerably. This increase was caused in part by a concerted program to privatize land holdings, which was implemented in 1991.

A woman takes a break from her work in a vineyard. While Armenia is well-known for its wines among the former Soviet republics, the rest of the world is just beginning to have access to them.

TOBACCO

Tobacco comes from the species *Nicotiana*. As its name suggests, nicotine, an addictive substance, is found in this species, concentrated in its leaves. The leaves, once cured, are used for smoking (in cigarettes, cigars, and pipes), chewing, as snuff, and for the extraction of nicotine, which is also an ingredient of products such as insecticides. The common tobacco plant is usually cultivated to a height of about 3–4 feet (1 meter), although if left unpruned, it can grow to as high as 10 feet (3 meters). Its leaves branch out from a central stem to a length ranging from 3 inches (9 cm) in some varieties to 3 feet (1 meter) in others.

Armenia is one of many countries with soil and climatic conditions suitable for tobacco cultivation. Even then, the growth process is labor-intensive, and a great deal of care goes into producing quality tobacco. Each tobacco variety has its own moisture and fertilizing requirements. Seedlings are germinated in boxes before being transplanted to the field. Tobacco plants grown for the fine thin leaves used to wrap around cigars must be cultivated under a cloth canopy. Harvesting by hand occurs in stages. Harvested leaves are dried and then cured by air, fire, or heat. The method used affects the aroma and flavor of the tobacco.

After curing, the leaves are graded by factors such as color, size, and their position on the main stem; lower leaves have less nicotine. The different grades of leaves are packed in bales and shipped to tobacco warehouses for auction.

INDUSTRY

In the heavy industry sector, Armenia specializes in machine-building—especially machine tools, presses, and foundry equipment—and chemical production. During the late 1960s, chemical production was a major industry for Armenia. Although the country is doing well in both these industries even today, it produces no raw materials to support the industries.

Brandy (below) and other liqueurs are among Armenia's export products.

The light industry sector accounts for more than a fourth of Armenia's total industrial output. Clothing and footwear, as well as other consumer durables such as canned foods, account for the bulk of the light industry output.

Although the clothing industry accounts for a significant percentage of industrial output, Armenia does not produce enough cotton fabrics, wool, woollen yarn, and silk to support its clothing industry. As a result, raw material for the clothing industry is imported. The end products—knitwear and ready-made garments—are primarily for export.

Armenia also produces several consumer durable goods such as radios, washing machines, freezers, refrigerators, and bicycles. However, Armenia's production of the more popular consumer durables—such as television sets, stereos, vacuum cleaners, and furniture—does not meet domestic demand.

While still under Soviet rule, Armenia was an important center for scientific research. It still produces computers, calculators, measuring instruments, and semiconductor-related items.

Vanadzor's central heating plant, powered by nuclear energy.

MINING AND ENERGY

Armenia has a fairly healthy cache of mineral resources, including marble, basalt, granite, tufa, lead, zinc, gold, copper, and silver. Iron ore is also mined. Mineral products include soda. The country is a major source of molybdenum, aluminum, and rare metals such as selenium and tellurium. Armenia is also a producer of mineral water.

Semiprecious and precious stones account for the highest percentage of total mineral exports. A large portion of these are thought to be rough diamonds imported into Armenia for finishing. Armenians are known for their skill in jewelry craftsmanship.

Although it has not officially been proven, studies indicate that Armenia has reserves of about six billion barrels of oil and six trillion cubic feet of natural gas. In addition, it is also estimated that there are 100 million tons of coal in the country.

The country is highly dependent on energy supplies from Russia and Turkmenistan. The production of domestic energy fell sharply after the Chernobyl disaster and the 1988 earthquake. The situation became critical in 1991 when Azerbaijan closed off the main pipeline transporting Russian gas to Armenia. At the moment, a secondary pipeline running through Georgia is the only external source of gas for the country.

Severe shortage has forced the Armenian government to seek alternative energy sources. Armenia signed an agreement in May 1995 to construct a pipeline for liquefied petroleum gas supplies from Iran. This pipeline will also be used to carry natural gas from Turkmenistan through Iran and Armenia to the European markets.

TRANSPORTATION AND COMMUNICATION

Armenia has about 520 miles (840 km) of railroad with links to Turkey, Iran, Georgia, and Russia. The main highway to Georgia passes through Azerbaijan while the reconstruction of a bridge over the Araks River has improved road access to Iran, facilitating the supply of consumer goods. A large portion of the roads (about 40 percent), are in need of repair.

The ban of a leading opposition political party, the Dashnaks, in 1994 led to the shutting down of 11 newspapers thought to be affiliated with the party in some way. There are other newspapers, but difficulty in gaining access to printing facilities frequently results in national newspapers being printed on an irregular basis. Both television and radio are state-owned, but an independent high-frequency radio station is in operation.

Telecommunications in Armenia is still in its infancy. There are approximately eight telephones for every 100 people. Telecommunications infrastructure development has largely been focused in Yerevan, which has about 45 percent of the total number of telephones. In rural areas, telecommunications services are almost nonexistent.

As a result of Azerbaijan's economic blockade, Armenians had to wait in long lines to buy gas for their cars.

ARMENIANS

ARMENIANS ARE ONE of the oldest races in history. They are the contemporaries of Babylonians, Hittites, and Assyrians, and a host of other ancient races.

Armenians call themselves "Hai" and claim descent from Haik, the great grandson of Japeth, son of Noah. Haik challenged the authority of Belus, the despot of Babylon, killed him in combat, and gathering his family, settled on what later was to be known as the home of the Armenians. This was the beginning of the Armenian state (c. 1200 B.C.).

History shows that the Armenian advance from Cappadocia to the plateau of Erzerum near Mt. Ararat (present-day eastern Turkey) took place between the seventh and eighth centuries B.C. The tribes living in these districts were either absorbed by the Armenians or fled to the north of the Caucasus.

Armenians are considered the most dynamic of the peoples of the former Soviet Union. They have an outstanding economic growth rate and standards in education and medical science on par with Western Europe. A long history of repeated invasions have created a people with toughness and endurance.

Left: **An Armenian family spending their Sunday together visiting the 13th century Astvatsatsin Church.**

Opposite: **This woman has likely lived through three Armenias—Turkish Armenia, Soviet Armenia, and now independent Armenia.**

A SOCIABLE PEOPLE

Armenia's population is about 3.7 million. Almost 70 percent of the population lives in urban areas. About 51 percent of the population is female. Age-wise, Armenia's population is in good shape, with the bulk of it (56.2 percent) in the 17–59 age range.

The people of Armenia are the product of a process of ethnic mingling that has been going on for thousands of years in Transcaucasia, due mainly to the many foreign invasions in that area.

Growing up in independent Armenia, these sisters' adult life will probably be more Westernized than that of their parents.

Most Armenians are dark-haired and dark-eyed, stocky in build, and of medium height. Armenians generally have prominent noses—sometimes aquiline, sometimes bulbous in shape. Physically, they bear a closer resemblance to the ancient inhabitants of Asia Minor than to the Scythians or other Indo-European nomads from southern Russia.

As a people, Armenians are extremely sociable and hospitable, and faithful to family and community ties. They are deeply attached to their national church and most Armenians have a pronounced religious bent. They can often seem serious and subdued in manner, but this does not render them devoid of humor. It has been said of Armenians that their distinguishing characteristic is grit, to which they owe their continued existence as a people.

VICTOR AMBARTSUMIAN

Armenia has produced its share of prominent personalities in the arts, sports, and academia. Victor Ambartsumian (1908–1996) was one such person.

Born in Tbilisi, Georgia, Ambartsumian was a prominent astrophysicist who challenged conventional thinking. He suggested that many of the processes involved in the creation and evolution of the universe and of individual galaxies occur during the dispersion and decrease in the density of matter. He demonstrated that galaxies are surrounded by clusters of distinct star types which are unstable and so young that they must still be forming in areas of expansion and density. Ambartsumian also challenged conventional theories when he disputed the idea that certain stars were formed as a product of galactic collision. He claimed

that they were produced through colossal explosions in the nuclei of normal galaxies.

Born to an eminent Armenian philologist father, Victor Ambartsumian inherited his father's brilliant academic mind. He graduated from the Leningrad State University in 1928 in mathematics and physics and then went on to the Pulkovo Observatory to do his doctorate, which he received in 1931. Ambartsumian was appointed to a lectureship at Leningrad and after just three years was made a professor. But the ideological political climate in Russia at that time was unfavorable, and Ambartsumian and his team found themselves in conflict with the director of the Pulkovo Observatory. After much dispute, it was destroyed.

By the 1940s, the Russian government had decided to invest in science as a tool to shore up Communist ideologies, and a new era of Soviet research began. Ambartsumian was appointed head of astrophysics at Yerevan University in Armenia. Here he saw to the construction of the Byurakan Observatory which sits 13,000 feet (4,000 m) high on Mt. Aragats. (In the picture above, he is speaking to an international audience outside the observatory.)

Ambartsumian was a man of strong convictions and beliefs. In 1989, he went on a three-week hunger strike in an attempt to draw public and government attention to the conflict in Nagorno-Karabakh. He was twice awarded Russia's highest honor, the Hero of Socialist Labor medal, and after the collapse of the Soviet Union, he was awarded the National Hero of Armenia medal.

ARMENIANS ABROAD

Armenia's long and peppered history of invasions has resulted, unsurprisingly, in the exodus of Armenians from the country to avoid persecution or simply to escape conquest. Armenian colonies are found in virtually every corner of the globe, from the Americas to Europe and Asia.

Today, Armenians in the former Soviet Union, Western Europe, and in the United States have risen to the top of all the arts and scientific professions. Armenians are found in key positions in medicine and physics, in school and university teaching and research, and in literature and music.

Victor Ambartsumian is a world-renowned astrophysicist; William Saroyan claims international fame as novelist and storyteller; Aram Khatchaturian is a household name in operatic and orchestral music; and Charles Aznavour is a popular figure in light music and song. The London musical scene is enriched by Armenian violinist Manoug Parikian and by the talented music criticism of Felix Aprahamian, while in Europe and America, operatic stages pay homage to the voices of prima donnas Lynne Dourian and Luisa-Anais Bosabalian. Singapore's world-famous Raffles Hotel, which entertained such distinguished guests as Somerset Maugham, was built and originally owned by Armenian entrepreneurs, the Sarkies brothers.

Popular French singer Charles Aznavour is of Armenian descent.

ARMENIANS IN ISTANBUL

Prior to 1453, the year Fatih Sultan Mehmet conquered Constantinople (modern Istanbul, Turkey), few Armenians resided in the Byzantine capital. In fact, after Sultan Mehmet's conquest, many Armenian inhabitants fled the city. The population of the city then was 40,000, the majority of whom were Greeks. In an effort to augment the population of that city, Mehmet ordered his administrators to bring people from all areas of Anatolia. Many were brought by force, and many of these were Armenians.

Although there were people of many different races and faiths living in the Ottoman empire—Armenians, Turks, and other Asians, who were Muslims, Christians, or Jews—the Armenian community was considered the most loyal among them all. The Turkish authorities called the Armenian community *millet-i sadika* ("MIL-ay-ee SAH-dee-KAH"), which in Turkish means "the loyal nation." Their loyalty saw many Armenians serving the Ottoman government and army.

The exact population of Armenians in Istanbul is not known as many do not register themselves. It is estimated that some 60,000 Armenians are currently residing in the city. Very few Armenians live in other parts of Turkey.

Armenian-American writer William Saroyan was awarded the Pulitzer Prize in 1940 for his play *The Time of Your Life.*

THE MINORITIES

The minority races in Armenia enjoy equal rights and freedom to practice their religion and culture, rights which are clearly defined in the country's Declaration of Independence. The government has adopted policies encouraging the minority communities to develop their own culture and educate their communities.

Russians currently make up the largest minority population in Armenia. Apart from them, there are also Kurds and Yezidis, who live mainly in the rural areas in Armenia. Though the language spoken by Yezidis is Kurdish, they tend to regard themselves as distinct from the Kurds.

The Kurdish community in Armenia is also very active. There is a Kurdological Department of the Institute of Oriental Studies at the Yerevan State University and a Kurdish Writers Union of Armenia. In addition, Yerevan has been a center of Kurdish publishing activity for some decades, as well as the center for Kurdish broadcasting, not only to Kurds in Armenia and the rest of Transcaucasia, but also to Kurds abroad, primarily in Turkey and Iran.

After seven decades of Soviet rule, many Jews are also coming forward to assert their Jewish identity. The Jewish community in Armenia dates back to the first century A.D., when Tigran the Great resettled 10,000 Jews in Armenia following his retreat from Palestine. The most recent wave of Jews arrived during World War II as Armenia offered a safe haven for those driven away from the Nazi-occupied areas of Russia, Belarus, and Ukraine.

The Jewish community in Armenia has its own cultural center. About 200 students, half of whom are adults, attend its Sunday school.

KURDS

"Kurd" is the ethnic name of a number of tribal groups inhabiting the mountainous border regions of southeast Turkey, northwest Iran, north Iraq, northeast Syria, rural Armenia, and Azerbaijan. These tribes speak various dialects of Kurdish, an Indo-Iranian language. They call their rugged homeland Kurdistan. Most Kurds are Sunni Muslims.

Kurds resemble neighboring southwest Asian populations except that they tend to show a somewhat higher incidence of fair coloring. Reliable statistics are lacking, but their number is estimated at 25 million, most of which are in Turkey (52%), Iraq (18%), and Iran (24%).

Most Kurds live in rural villages, cultivating wheat, barley, cotton, and fruit. Some are nomads, but these have dwindled since the closing of national frontiers and the Kurdish political struggles of the last several decades. The traditional Kurdish tribal system follows a patrilineal structure, and the leaders have great status.

Although the Kurds have never been united politically, Kurdish autonomy has had a long history. "Kurd" as a collective name was first applied to the tribal groups in the seventh century A.D. when they converted to Islam. Three short-lived Kurdish dynasties existed in the 10th to 12th centuries. The 12th century Kurdish warrior Saladin, a prominent foe of the Crusaders, founded another dynasty that lasted into the 13th century. During succeeding centuries numerous Kurdish principalities vied for local power, showing little interest in achieving unity. Only in the late 19th and early 20th centuries did a nationalist movement emerge. With the breakup of the Ottoman empire after World War I, Turkey agreed to the establishment of an independent Kurdistan under the Treaty of Sevres (1920). This part of the treaty was never ratified, however, and the autonomy clause was completely eliminated from the Treaty of Lausanne (1923) through Turkish efforts under Kemal Ataturk.

Kurds in Iran launched an unsuccessful uprising after the 1979 Islamic revolution, and Kurdish separatist guerrillas remain active in Turkey despite Turkish efforts to assimilate the nation's Kurdish population, but most nationalist activity since 1946 has been in Iraq. There Kurds waged guerrilla warfare in 1961–1970 and open rebellion in 1974–1975 against the Iraqi government. This movement collapsed when unofficial Iranian support was withdrawn after a 1975 Iran-Iraq border accord. Iraqi Kurdish separatists later backed Iran in the Iran-Iraq war of 1980–1988. In 1988, the Iraqi government was accused of using chemical weapons against the Kurds. Iraqi Kurds again revolted after Iraq's defeat in the 1991 Persian Gulf War. When the rebellion failed, more than a million of them fled their homes. As the death toll among the Kurds mounted, U.S. military forces built camps for them in northern Iraq. The administration of these camps was later assumed by the United Nations. In April 1992, Iraqi Kurds held their first elections free of Iraqi control to choose a leader and a Kurdish National Assembly. More than 100,000 Iraqi Kurds are thought to have been killed since the mid-1970s, however, and the Kurdish zone in northern Iraq remains under an Iraqi economic blockade. The Kurds there fear further attacks by Iraqi military forces.

LIFESTYLE

ARMENIA PLACES A HIGH PRIORITY on educating its population. According to official statistics, 90 percent of Armenia's population is literate. Armenia has a well-developed system of higher educational institutions and scientific research and technological institutes. This network has been instrumental in supporting the development of several high-tech industries in Armenia.

The Ter-Petrossian administration's emphasis on educating the population has produced results—almost 15 percent of the population has had at least eight years of education, 44 percent has had at least 10 years of education, and 13 percent has graduated with a degree from one of the many universities in the country. Many Armenians also go abroad for postgraduate education.

Left: **Armenian women living in the countryside fetching water from a pipe by a railway station.**

Opposite: **An Armenian woman selling sunflower seeds. Many older Armenians supplement their family's income by selling foodstuff on the street.**

A computer class. Until the early 1990s, Armenia's general education system conformed to the centralized Soviet system. Since independence, extensive changes have been introduced, with greater emphasis on Armenian history and culture.

EDUCATION

Education, which has always played a central role in Armenia, is compulsory and free at elementary and high school levels. Children aged 6 to 16 must have at least 8 to 10 years of schooling. After that, they have an option of going to college or to vocational school.

The language medium in institutions of higher learning is Armenian, although Russian is also taught. There are 25 public institutions of higher education (including seven colleges) and 40 private educational institutions.

The leading educational institutions, such as the Yerevan State University, the Yerevan State Medical University, the Yerevan State Institute for Russian and Foreign Languages, and the Yerevan Komitas Conservatory, are recognized for outstanding achievements in their fields.

Armenia's high educational standards have given rise to many inventions by Armenian scientists and engineers. From 1980 to 1990, 4,300 inventions were patented by Armenians, amounting to about 22 inventions per 1,000 researchers per year. Armenian researchers have developed many internationally marketable technologies. One successful product developed in the Armenian Academy of Science is a baby food called Narine, which has therapeutic and nutritive qualities and was licensed to the Japanese Miki Trading Company.

HUMAN RIGHTS

The Armenian government has adopted international conventions on human, civil, and political rights, as well as universal standards of freedom of conscience and religion. This is clearly stated in the second chapter of Armenia's constitution.

Concern over human rights in Armenia, however, was heightened upon the suspension in 1995 of the Armenian Revolutionary Federation (ARF), one of several opposition parties in Armenia. In May 1995, an ARF prisoner died while in state custody. This prompted ARF party members to accuse the Ter-Petrossian administration of severe abuse of political prisoners and harassment of opposition members. The Armenian government has also been accused of violating the human rights guarantees in the Armenian constitution as well as the international human rights conventions that it has adopted.

A class outing to a memorial statue commemorating Armenia's independence. Having been subjugated and persecuted for much of their long history, Armenians included human rights guarantees in their constitution.

Other detainees have also accused the government of torture and of intimidation and harassment of their families and lawyers. Several publications and opposition newspapers in the country have been shut down.

The Ter-Petrossian administration, however, insists this is only a temporary measure. Both Amnesty International and Human Rights Watch have expressed concern about human rights in Armenia.

HEALTH AND SOCIAL WELFARE

A considerable portion of Armenia's health and social welfare system is still predominantly financed from the state budget. Much of Armenia's expenditure on health and welfare services has been directed towards the victims of the 1988 earthquake, which killed an estimated 25,000 people and caused US$5 billion worth of damage. Armenia's conflict with Azerbaijan over the territory of Nagorno-Karabakh, coupled with the collapse of the Soviet Union, also saw the migration of a large number of refugees into Armenia, creating new demands on social expenditure and putting more pressure on the national budget.

A hospital in Armenia. Armenia's health care system is supplemented by medical aid from humanitarian organizations.

Although the health care budget saw a small increase from 8 percent of the total budget in 1992 to 13.5 percent in 1994, this has still proved insufficient to meet the needs of Armenians. Current allocations are sufficient only to pay for wages and public utilities. In addition, many rural clinics and district hospitals that are financed from a local district budget are now in a serious state of disrepair. Currently, about 70 percent of medical equipment and medicine, baby formula, and vaccines for infants is donated by international humanitarian organizations.

Armenia's birth rate has been declining over the past few years. According to clinical observations, the physical characteristics of newborn children have noticeably deteriorated, with an alarming increase in the number of children born underweight.

Armenians' life expectancy at birth is 71.2 years. The women have an average life expectancy of 74.4 years while for men, it is 67.9 years.

ARMENIAN REFUGEES

Armenia's continuing conflict with Azerbaijan has created a community of refugees in Armenia. In 1988, Nagorno-Karabakh, a predominantly ethnic Armenian enclave within Azerbaijan, voted to secede and join Armenia. Armenian support for the separatists led to an economic blockade by Azerbaijan (joined by Turkey), which crippled Armenia's foreign trade and restricted imports of food and fuel. This blockade is still in place today.

Ethnic Azeris who fled or were deported from Armenia in 1988 and 1989 remain refugees primarily in Azerbaijan. Armenia, in turn, has received the lion's share of the roughly 400,000 ethnic Armenians who have fled Azerbaijan since 1988. Many of these refugees are still living in temporary houses and refugee camps. Providing for them has put an enormous burden on Armenia's already overtaxed welfare budget.

Thousands of Armenian refugees are housed in temporary shelters.

In cities, many grandmothers double as daycare providers for their grandchildren while their daughters are at work.

WOMEN IN ARMENIA

Women in Armenia have come a long way since independence. While women living in the rural areas may still be somewhat traditional and play roles limited to looking after families and bearing children, urban women have started to foray into the labor market. Part of the reason for this is that the cost of living in the cities is higher, necessitating a two-income family.

The lot of urban working women in Armenia is similar to that of working women in other countries. Although many work full-time to help augment the family income, the main burden of housework and child care still rests firmly on their shoulders.

The advent of women into the labor market and its attendant problems of what to do with the children and issues of unequal pay and the glass ceiling have resulted in the creation of many women's groups. One of the most well-known and successful is Shamiram, which now has eight

SHAMIRAM

Shamiram, or the Armenian Women's Union, was founded in April 1995 to champion and safeguard women's rights and increase the involvement of women in the fields of policy, decisionmaking, and democratic and market reforms. The party's aim is to improve and expand social programs, medical care, and education for all Armenians. The group is also strongly against the current tax policy, which is considered an overwhelming burden for the average Armenian household.

Eight out of the 12 women deputies in the National Assembly are Shamiram members, namely Zaruhi Arevshatian, Anzhela Bakunts, Juliet Kazhoyan, Shogher Matevosian, Amalya Petrosian, Nadezhda Sargisian, Gayane Sarukhanian, and Anahit Torosian.

Shogher Matevosian heads Shamiram, and the party is estimated to have a membership of about 4,400 women.

members as deputies in the National Assembly. In spite of their double burden of career and household duties, many Armenian women, like opera singers Gohar Gasparian and pianist Svetlana Navasardian, have made an impact in the international arena.

Two women visiting with each other after having attended to their household chores.

NATIONAL DRESS

The Armenian national dress has several variations, depending on what area of Armenia the wearer is from. Generally, Armenian women wear long skirts with an apron under an ornately trimmed blouse, or a kaftan.

Women in Armenian dress with traditional offerings of food and drink. Armenian national dress is usually worn only on special occasions.

Some women wear wide trousers. The women also wear elaborate jewelry and headgear. Their shoes or boots have toes pointing upward.

Men generally wear wide trousers, a long-sleeved waistcoat, and some kind of turban. The men's boots also turn up at the toe end.

The traditional dress of Yezidi women from the area around Gyumri in the northwest consists of a red velvet unlined garment with a velvet apron, lined with printed calico. The hem of the dress and the edges of the apron are usually trimmed with a zigzag design. An ornate quilted piece made of pieces of colored silk adorned with glass beads and buttons is tied to the chest with strings around the neck and waist. High soft leather boots decorated with appliqué and impressed designs are worn over ankle-high leather shoes.

Women from northwest Armenia wear kaftans made of coarse striped silk decorated with thin gold braid around the neckline. The front of the kaftan is edged with silk-covered buttons. The long sleeves are further lengthened with false sleeves in a contrasting color to imitate an undergarment. The false sleeves are also cut in a zigzag pattern and decorated with gold braid. The caps that these women wear have long silk tassels.

Women from this region also wear short silk damask jackets edged with gold cord trimming over wide trousers. The sleeves of the jacket end in a point. The trousers are generally made of a coarser silk than the jacket. The leather slippers that they wear, with the toes pointing upward, are embroidered in red.

Part of the traditional dress of a male Kurd from the Yerevan area is wide trousers elaborately trimmed with silk and gold cord. These are fastened around the waist with a drawstring. The sleeved waistcoat that they wear is styled after the kaftan and almost always of a striped fabric, closing with small buttons at the neck. Gold braid is sometimes added down the front to give the impression of an ornate fastening.

A woman in 16th century Armenian dress. Traditional Armenian clothes have changed relatively little over the centuries.

RELIGION

CHRISTIANITY IS THE dominant religion in Armenia. Most Armenian Christians belong to the Armenian Church, but there is also a sizable Russian Orthodox minority. The other large minority religion is Islam, although Muslims have dwindled due to the departure of most Azerbaijanis.

Prior to the adoption of Christianity as the state religion in A.D. 301, Armenian beliefs were reflected by the religions prevalent in the Mediterranean and Eastern Europe.

During the fifth century B.C., while under the Persian empire, Armenians adopted the Persian gods and domesticated them. Ahura-Mazda, father of the gods, was worshiped as Aramazd, while Mithra, god of light and justice, was known as Mihr. Anahita, goddess of fertility and mother of all wisdom, became Anahit, the favorite goddess of the Armenians.

Under Alexander the Great, Armenia entered the Hellenistic orbit and adopted the Greek pantheon of gods. Early Greek priests brought statues of their gods to Armenia and placed them in Hellenistic temples. As a result, a Persian-Greco religion as well as the worship of local spirits existed until the adoption of Christianity in the fourth century.

The Armenian Apostolic Church, established by the apostles Thaddeus and Bartholomew, preserves its national exclusiveness, recognizes the supremacy of no other spiritual jurisdiction, and considers itself the equal of the churches in Rome and Istanbul.

Opposite: **The richly adorned throne of St. James the Less in the Armenian Cathedral in Jerusalem, one of the two patriarchates of the Armenian Church (the other is in Istanbul, Turkey).**

Below: **Although Armenia is the first state to adopt Christianity as a national religion, some older customs have persisted. For example, in ancient times, Armenians considered trees to be sacred plants with the power to grant special favors and requests. By tying strips of cloth to a tree, one could ask for help or heal sick relatives and friends. Some Armenians continue this practice today.**

Echmiadzin Cathedral is the spiritual center of the Armenian Church and the seat of the Catholicos of all Armenians. It is also the oldest cathedral and Christian monastery in the world.

THE ARMENIAN APOSTOLIC CHURCH

The Armenian Church is one of the oldest churches in Christendom. The Gospel was preached in Armenia by the apostles Thaddeus and Bartholomew in the first century, establishing the apostolic origins of their church.

Armenian martyrologies carry the names of many Christian bishops dating back to the first century. The names of some of these martyrs are included in the Ecclesiastical History of Eusebius of Caesarea (*c.* A.D. 260–340), who is regarded as the first historian of Christianity.

The Armenian Church retained its independent status. When the great Council of Nicaea was held in A.D. 325 to establish a common creed, 318 bishops attended, each representing an independent church of equal status. Armenia was represented by Aristakes, a son and successor of Gregory the Illuminator.

Its independent position served to separate the Armenian Church from the Chalcedonian churches (that is, the churches represented at the Council of Chalcedon in A.D. 451) and preserved its individuality. It also caused great conflict with the Byzantine Church, which frequently

ST. GREGORY CHURCH IN SINGAPORE

St. Gregory Church is Singapore's oldest church and only Armenian church. The church was founded in 1835 by 12 Armenian merchant families who settled on the island. In Singapore, the church is famous for the fact that it was the first to be provided with electric lighting, in 1909.

In 1994, the 160-year-old church underwent renovation and repair in order to conserve it. (The gravestones pictured here were included in this renovation.) The church was reopened on December 25, 1994. Bishop Oshagan Choloyan, who flew in from Kuwait, conducted a service during the festive season that year.

The Armenian Church has been the Armenian people's unifying force throughout centuries of foreign invasion, occupation, and forced migration. Christianity remained strong in Armenia despite many efforts to stifle its expression. The Armenian Church combined nationalism and religion as its policy for safeguarding Armenian culture.

resorted to persecution and mass deportations in attempts to bring the Armenians in line. Later, during the period of the Cilician kingdom of the Armenians and at the time of the Crusades, this independence brought the Armenians into contention with the Roman Catholic Church. In more modern times, it has tended to separate the Armenians from the Russian Orthodox Church and the Czarist government.

As a national institution, the Armenian Apostolic Church has played an important role in Armenian history, at times assuming both political and spiritual leadership. The Church adopts this dual role even today.

The fall of the ruling dynasty during the fifth century may have ended the Armenian kingdom, but the head of the Church became the enduring symbol of national unity and the rallying point of patriotism. Through the centuries, Armenians at home and abroad have regarded the Catholicos of Echmiadzin not only as the head of their church but also as their spokesperson and elected representative.

Liturgy and ritual are very important aspects of the practice of the Armenian Church.
(Right) The patriarch of the Armenian Cathedral in Jerusalem.
(Below) A family lighting candles in church.

CHURCH RITUALS AND HIERARCHY

The Armenian Church places great importance on the liturgy, which has remained virtually unchanged since the 10th century. The liturgical music with characteristically Armenian notations dates to the 11th century. The

entire service, except the sermon—which is usually brief and considered less important—is in the modern vernacular.

The Holy Orders of the Armenian Church are the Diaconate, Priesthood, and Episcopate. Deacons and parish priests may marry, but they must do so before they are ordained. All other orders are celibate, including *vardapets* ("VAHR-dah-pets"), who are monastical priests. Bishops are chosen from this rank. The Episcopate, the highest rank,

CATHOLICOS OF ALL ARMENIANS

The title of Catholicos of all Armenians is the highest title to be bestowed in the Armenian Church. The Catholicos is elected by the National Religious Assembly.

The current Catholicos of all Armenians is Archbishop Karekin I, baptised Neshan Sarkissian. He succeeded Vazgen I, who died in August 1994. Karekin I was appointed the 131st Catholicos of all Armenians on April 4, 1995. He was born in Syria on August 27, 1932.

Karekin I was admitted to the Theological Seminary of the Armenian Catholicate of Cilicia in 1946, graduating with high honors in 1952. He joined the Theological Seminary in Antelias, Lebanon, first as a faculty member and later as dean. Karekin I's other key roles include being aide to Khoren I, Catholicos of the Great House of Cilicia. In 1963, in recognition of his service to the Church, he was made senior archmandrite. In 1964, he was made bishop and in 1973 he was made archbishop. During his term as archbishop, he served the Church in many capacities in the Middle East and in North America.

Karekin I's predecessor, Vazgen I, was instrumental in reestablishing faith among the Armenians in the Armenian Church. In an effort to improve relations between local and immigrant Armenians, he made many pastoral visits to the Armenian diaspora and forged strong links with other Christian churches. Under Archbishop Vazgen's leadership, 80 percent of Armenian children were baptized and over 50 percent attended church.

consists of bishops and archbishops, the Patriarchs of Constantinople (Istanbul) and Jerusalem, the Catholicos of Cilicia, and the Supreme Patriarch and Catholicos of all Armenians.

The Supreme Patriarch's seat is the Holy See of Echmiadzin, near Yerevan. His authority is universal throughout Armenia and the diaspora. However, for historical reasons the Catholicos of Cilicia has maintained separate jurisdictions since the 15th century, which now include Armenian churches in Syria, Lebanon, Iran, and Greece, and two prelacies in the United States. The Supreme Patriarch exercises authority and leadership through the two patriarchs and through prelates (archbishops and bishops) elected locally and confirmed by him in their respective diocese.

ORTHODOXY

The original Christian Church was founded by the apostles in the first century A.D. The churches of the East, commonly known as "Orthodox," hold true to the original dogma established by the universal church in the early centuries. "Orthodoxy" is from the Greek *orthodoxia*, which means "right opinion."

Ultimately five great sees were given the designation of patriarchate. These were Rome, Constantinople, Alexandria, Antioch, and Jerusalem. Rome was designated first, in recognition of the fact that this was the seat of secular power at the outset of Christianity; Constantinople was designated next when this became the seat of the Holy Roman empire, Emperor Constantine having decided in A.D. 324 to shift his capital from Rome to Byzantium; Alexandria and Antioch were designated as they were seats of great learning; and Jerusalem, although much smaller in extent and influence, was included as a special mark of respect for the Holy Land.

Bishops attended and participated as equals in periodic councils—the Councils of Nicaea (A.D. 325) and Chalcedon (A.D. 451) are two examples. Major decisions, including those on dogma, doctrine, and heresies, were made at these councils.

RUSSIAN ORTHODOX CHURCH

Orthodox priests in front of their church. The Russian Orthodox Church is the largest minority religion in Armenia.

Members of the Russian Orthodox Church make up the largest religious minority in Armenia. The Church, which marked its 1,008th anniversary in 1996, is the largest and most influential of all Orthodox churches.

The origin of the Russian Church dates back to the "baptism of Russia" in A.D. 988. The Russian Church was originally headed by Byzantine metropolitans appointed by the patriarch of Constantinople.

In 1448, the independence of the Russian Church was proclaimed. It was then headed by metropolitans elected by a council of Russian hierarchs, who did not have to be approved by the patriarch of Constantinople.

The title of patriarch was abolished in 1721 when Czar Peter the Great failed to get the support of the patriarch for his reforms. Peter replaced the role of the patriarch with the Holy Governing Synod, whose members were appointed by the czar, and the Synod administered the Russian Church. This system was abolished in 1917 when the Local Council of 1917–1918 restored the patriarchate.

ISLAM

The Muslim community in Armenia makes up one to two percent of the total population. Islam is practised by the Kurdish community and, to a lesser extent, by the Yezidis.

The word "Islam" in Arabic means "to surrender," but as a religious term in the Koran, it means "to surrender to the will or law of God." It was through Prophet Mohammed—who first began to preach a series of revelations granted to him by Allah (Arabic for "God")—that Islam was first introduced. The two fundamental sources of Islamic doctrine and practice are the Koran and the Sunna.

Muslims regard the Koran as the word of God as told to Mohammed, through Gabriel, the angel of revelation. They believe that God himself, not Mohammed, is the author and therefore the Koran is infallible. The Koran is the collection of the passages revealed to Mohammed during the approximately 22 years of his prophetic life (610–632).

The second substantive source of Islam, the Sunna, or example of the Prophet, is known through Hadith, the body of traditions based on what the Prophet said or did regarding various issues. Unlike the Koran, which was memorized by early Muslims during their lifetime and was compiled in written form quite early, the transmission of Hadith was largely verbal, and the present authoritative collections date from the ninth century.

Unlike the Koran, Hadith is not considered infallible. During the early days of Islam, whether the Prophet himself was infallible (apart from the revelations in the Koran) was a point of controversy. Later, however, the consensus of the Islamic community was that both he and the earlier prophets were infallible. Because Hadith was mainly transmitted orally, however, it was conceded that error could enter into the human transmission. Hadith, therefore, is a source secondary to the Koran.

While the majority of the population of Armenia (about 94 percent) are members of the Armenian Apostolic Church, there is also a small community belonging to the Russian Orthodox Church. Apart from that, there are Yezidis who practice Zoroastrianism, Christianity, and Islam, and a small community of Jews.

JUDAISM

The Jews are few in number in Armenia and represent the smallest minority group in the country.

Judaism originated in Israel. As a rich and complex religious tradition, Judaism has certain characteristic features. The most essential of these is a radical monotheism—that is, the belief that a single, transcendent God created the universe as we know it and continues to govern it. Supporting this monotheism is the belief that the world is both intelligible and purposive, because a single divine intelligence stands behind it. Therefore, nothing that humanity experiences is capricious; everything ultimately has meaning.

The mind of God is manifest to the traditional Jew in both the natural order, through creation, and the social-historical order, through revelation. Jews believe that the same God who created the world revealed himself to the Israelites at Mt. Sinai. The content of that revelation is the Torah (meaning "revealed instruction" in Hebrew), God's will for humankind expressed in commandments by which individuals are to regulate their lives in interacting with one another and with God. Only by living in accordance with God's laws and submitting to the divine will can humanity become a harmonious part of the cosmos.

A second major concept in Judaism is that of the covenant (*berith*)— meaning "contractual agreement"—between God and the Jewish people. According to tradition, the God of creation entered into a special relationship with the Jews at Sinai. The Jews would acknowledge God as their sole, ultimate king and legislator, agreeing to obey his laws; God, in turn, would acknowledge Israelites as his chosen people and be especially mindful of them.

Both biblical authors and later Jewish tradition view the covenant (between God and the Jews) in a universal context. In their view, only after successive failures to establish a covenant with rebellious humanity did God turn to a particular segment of it. Israel is to be a "kingdom of priests," and the ideal social order it establishes in accordance with the divine laws is to be a model for the human race. Israel thus stands between God and humanity, representing each to the other.

ZOROASTRIANISM

Zoroastrians believe in one god, Ahura-Mazda. Zoroastrianism thrived under various Persian dynasties and at one point, the Persian empire spanned the entire "civilized" world—eastern Greece to northern India. Remnants of the religion were left in Europe, including the cult of Mithraism, derived from Zoroastrianism. It even became the unofficial religion of the Romans.

The religion and empire were devastated when Alexander invaded Persia. Many of their sacred texts were lost or destroyed, although large portions of the texts were later reproduced. The empire was rebuilt and thrived during the Sassanian period, but was once again defeated with the advent of Islam. With the Arab invasions, the Zoroastrians of Iran were forced to either convert to Islam or be executed. Many fled by land and sea to the west coast of India where they became known as *Parsis* (Persians). The Parsis in India began to flourish in the 17th and 18th centuries during the British occupation of India. Many of the wealthiest families were Parsis.

All Zoroastrians must wear the *sudra-kusti* ("SOOD-rah KOOS-ti"). The *sudra* is a white cotton tunic while the *kusti* is a woollen string worn around the waist on top of the *sudra*. The tying of the *kusti* is a part of the basic daily prayers of a Zoroastrian.

Dead bodies are placed in a specially consecrated structure, called the Tower of Silence, to be consumed by vultures. This practice reaffirms Zoroastrians' belief of not polluting the elements.

Prayers are only recited in the sacred language, Avesta. The Zoroastrian book of daily prayers is called the *Khordeh Avesta* (Selected Avesta). It is a collection of prayers selected from other major Avestan works such as Yasna, Visparad, Vendidad, and the Yasht literature.

Zoroastrianism was founded in ancient Persia by the prophet Zarathushtra, and is considered to be the world's first monotheistic religion.

LANGUAGE

THE OFFICIAL ADOPTION of Christianity by King Tiridates III in A.D. 301 inaugurated a new phase in the spiritual and intellectual life of the Armenian people. The advent of Christianity meant that the founders of the Armenian Church had to set themselves the task of translating the New Testament and essential prayer books into Armenian.

Previous to this, prayers and chants were conducted either in Greek or in Syriac, and largely by foreign preachers with little or no knowledge of the Armenian tongue. The Armenian language—called Haieren by the Armenians—is an independent branch of the Indo-European group.

A major obstacle to the task was the fact that the Armenian language was primarily an oral language and had, as yet, no alphabet of its own. The difficult but vital task of inventing the alphabet for the Armenian language was ultimately achieved in A.D. 405 by an Armenian monk, Mesrop Mashtotz.

With the alphabet evolved the classical Armenian language known as Grabar or "book language." The first work of literature with the new alphabet was the translation of the Bible from Greek. Thereafter, numerous literary works, both originals and translations, were written in Grabar.

But Grabar gradually lagged behind the developing national speech, although it prevailed for a long time in literature and church texts. Subsequently Grabar, incomprehensible to the mass of the people, fell into disuse. Ashkharabar, a new literary language, formed towards the 19th century, came into its own in literature and became the national language.

Below: **Manuscripts from Yerevan's Matenadaran Institute. The institute has approximately 116,000 manuscripts, including treatises in history, philosophy, law, medicine, mathematics, and geography as well as works of literature and miniature paintings.**

Opposite: **An engraving of the Armenian alphabet.**

THE ARMENIAN ALPHABET

The lack of an alphabet made it impossible for Armenians to have a literature of their own. As the Armenian state was challenged by foreign foes, it was necessary for the Armenians to have their own literature if they were to survive as a people. With the encouragement of Catholicos Sahag and King Vramshabouh, Mesrop Mashtotz devised an alphabet which had 36 letters. (Three were added later.)

The Armenian alphabet was devised to represent Armenian sounds. It is believed to have been influenced by Syriac (a form of Aramaic) and Pahlavi (a Persian language), and to a lesser extent, by Greek.

The original alphabet was written in large capital letters. Between the 10th and 11th centuries, a type of curved initials, called *boloragits yerkatagir* ("boh-loh-RAH-gitz yuhr-KAH-tah-GEER") or "iron capitals," were used. The "middle" *yerkatagir* of the 11th and 12th centuries had more straight lines, and there is also a lower-case *yerkatagir* script. Sometimes a combination of more than one style of *yerkatagir* occurs, referred to as "mixed letters."

Since the 13th century, the predominant script has been the small *bologir* ("boh-loh-GEER") writing, which closely resembles most Armenian printing of the present day. In the 18th century, a form of cursive writing was developed.

The invention of an Armenian alphabet allowed the translation of all the major works of the classical age and the writing of original Armenian works. This period was the Golden Age of Armenian literature. This cultural and religious work was accomplished just in time. Soon thereafter Armenia was divided by Rome and Persia, and the Armenian dynasty came to an end. Thanks to the Armenian alphabet and Armenian literature, however, the Armenian culture survived.

Learning a second language.

Towards the end of the 19th century 246 newspapers and journals were being published in Armenian all over the world. At the beginning of the 20th century this had increased to 724.

EASTERN AND WESTERN ARMENIAN

By the 19th century, two major Armenian dialects evolved that are still in use—Eastern Armenian and Western Armenian. Each dialect has two "r" sounds, three "ch" sounds, three "t" sounds, and two "p" sounds. In Western Armenian, some of the distinctions between the soft "t" and the middle "t" have disappeared; in Eastern Armenian, the sounds are distinct. The other difference lies in the conjugation of verbs. The present tense in Western Armenian looks like the future tense in Eastern Armenian.

The invention of the Armenian alphabet by Mesrop Mashtotz played a decisive role in preserving the national identity and culture of the Armenian people. In 1961, the 1,600th anniversary of Mashtotz's birth was observed by the whole of the Soviet Union.

MESROP MASHTOTZ

Mesrop Mashtotz (361–440), the creator of the Armenian alphabet, was born in the province of Taron. He graduated from one of the schools established by Catholicos Nerses the Great. A man of exceptional ability who had mastered Greek, Syriac, Persian, and other languages, Mashtotz was soon appointed a royal secretary at the city of Vagharshapat, or Echmiadzin, then the capital of Armenia. After a few years of government service, Mesrop resigned his post and entered the Church.

Around the age of 40, Mesrop began preaching in different parts of Armenia. It was in the course of these tours that he conceived the idea of inventing an Armenian alphabet with the objective of translating the Bible. He realized that this would both help propagate the Christian faith and establish a strong tie to bind together Armenians living in eastern and western Armenia and elsewhere. Mesrop and his pupils set to work and completed the task in A.D. 405.

The original set of characters in the alphabet that Mesrop and his disciples devised is still in use today, though written in modern, cursive script. This is a great tribute to the remarkable pioneer, who passed away at a ripe old age of 79.

Mashtotz is buried in the crypt of the church at Oshakan, not far from Echmiadzin. The shrine is guarded to this day by a lineal descendant of Mesrop's patron and protector, Vahan Amatuni.

OTHER LANGUAGES

The official language of the country is Armenian. However, Armenia's long association with the former Soviet Union has meant that many people in Armenia are well versed in written and spoken Russian.

Apart from that, some major Western languages, such as Spanish, Italian, German, French, and especially English are also included in the public school curriculum, and are extensively taught in most colleges and universities.

Part of the Indo-European family of Slavic languages, Russian uses the Cyrillic alphabet, which is made up of 33 letters. Spelling is basically, though not completely, phonetic, and the rules of pronunciation are few and simple.

The Russian language has no articles, either definite or indefinite. All Russian nouns fall into the three grammatical genders of the masculine, the feminine, and the neuter.

Adjectives agree with nouns in gender, case, and number. The verb has three tenses, present, past, and future; in addition it has the category of aspect. The two aspects are the imperfective, presenting the action as a process of repetition, and the perfective, presenting the action as a unified whole.

A billboard in Armenian and Azerbaijani.

A typical feature of Russian vocabulary is large families of words derived from the same root by means of adding various prefixes and suffixes.

THE WISE WEAVER—AN ARMENIAN FOLKTALE

One upon a time, the king was seated on his throne when an ambassador arrived from a distant land. Without saying a word, the ambassador drew a circle around the throne, then sat down and remained silent. The king was puzzled. He summoned all his counselors and asked them what the envoy meant. But none of them could give him an answer.

The king was upset and offended. Was there not a single wise man among his courtiers and advisers? He gave his courtiers strict orders to find a man in his kingdom wise enough to know the answer; otherwise he promised them that he would slay them all.

With the incentive of keeping their heads if they succeeded, the courtiers wasted no time going around the city looking for such a man. In a poor part of the city, they happened to enter a house where they saw a cradle with a baby in it rocking by itself. There was no one else in the house. They saw the same thing in the next house: the cradle rocking by itself and nobody in the building. When they went up to the roof they saw a stick moving by itself to frighten away the birds from the grain that was washed and spread out to dry in the sun.

The king's courtiers were amazed. They went down one floor below, where they saw a weaver working at his loom. He had a string tied to one end of the shuttle, a string to the other end, and a third string tied to the comb. As the shuttle moved back and forth over the loom, the two cradles and the stick set on the roof for frightening the birds away moved with it. A clever weaver indeed.

"An ambassador came from another land and drew a circle around the king's throne, but refuses to speak," the courtiers said to the weaver. "We do not know what he means. Maybe you know. Come with us. The king will reward you well if you can solve this puzzle."

The weaver thought it over for a moment, then agreed to go with the courtiers to the king's castle. But he said he had to get a few things first. He took a couple of knucklebones and a pullet and put them in his coat. Then he set off to the king's palace with the courtiers.

On reaching the palace, the weaver took out the knucklebones and threw them before the ambassador. The ambassador took a fistful of millet from his pocket and scattered it on the floor. At this, the weaver pulled out his pullet from under his coat and let it eat the grain.

The ambassador then stood up and departed, without saying a word.

The king and the courtiers were all amazed at this series of events. "What does it mean?" they asked the weaver.

"By drawing a circle around the king's throne, the ambassador meant that his king is coming to besiege our city," answered the weaver, "and he wanted to know whether our king would submit or fight. When I threw my knucklebones before him, I meant they should go and play with knucklebones—they are nothing but children to us, and it is foolish of them to pretend they could fight our king. By scattering the millet on the floor, he meant that his king has innumerable warriors at his command. However, when my pullet ate all the millet, the ambassador understood what I meant—that one of us can slaughter a thousand such warriors."

The king was so pleased with the weaver that he wanted to make him the new chamberlain. But the weaver respectfully declined, preferring to go back to his loom.

"But I implore you, O King," the weaver said, "not to forget that among your humblest servants there are men wiser than your counselors, and I hope from now on your courtiers will treat the weaver and the cobbler with respect."

ARTS

ARMENIA'S LONG HISTORY and mix of cultures has had a profound impact on its arts. Although much of Armenia's rich heritage in the arts extant today dates from A.D. 301, when Christianity became the state religion, the arts of pre-Christian Armenia are also significant, especially those from the ninth to sixth centuries B.C., when Armenia was part of the Urartu kingdom. The Urartians were major producers of bronze objects. Excavations at the Karmir-Blur, begun in 1939 and continuing today, have uncovered household utensils, furniture decorations, and pieces of military equipment such as helmets, arrows, and shields fashioned out of bronze. Urartian smiths were apparently also very skilled in silver and gold craft. Vases, medallions, and amulets were fashioned from silver while gold was used to create articles of jewelry. The Urartian smiths' specialty was decorating metal with mythological and animal forms.

Left: **Carving a *khatchkar*, or memorial stone, an Armenian specialty.**

Opposite: **A statue of David of Sassoun, a legendary Armenian hero, which stands outside Yerevan's main railway station.**

ARCHITECTURE

Churches provided the main form of architectural expression in early Armenia. The seventh century was the golden age of Armenian ecclesiastical architecture. A great many cathedrals and monuments with interior frescoes and stone carvings relating to Biblical stories were constructed.

The best known is the palace church of Zwartnotz, erected by Catholicos Nerses III of Ishkhan between 643 and 652. Now in ruins, the church was a circular domed structure 148 feet (45 m) high and 118 feet (36 m) in diameter. The pillars within had carvings of birds and intricate geometrical designs. The remains of the walls and the foundations can still be seen.

Although the Arab occupation of Armenia imposed a halt in church building, Arab (and Islamic) influence on Armenian architecture was apparent after the 10th century. The most renowned church built in this period is the Church of Aghtamar, on a small island at the southeastern corner of Lake Van. The chief glory of this building is its sculptures, which hold a central position in the art history of the Middle East and are important for the understanding of Christian and Islamic art of the period. Many of them bear a striking resemblance to themes found in contemporary Muslim art, for example, the Biblical king of Assyria dressed as a turbaned Arab prince.

The Church of Aghtamar on Lake Van (in present-day Turkey) is the best-known extant example of the Arab and Islamic influence on Armenian architecture.

Armenian architecture was also influenced by the West. Its grandest expression is the Ani Cathedral. Built by world famous Armenian architect Tiridates under the sponsorship of King Gagik I, its colossal dome is 100 feet (30 m) in diameter with a crown 180 feet (55 m) above the floor.

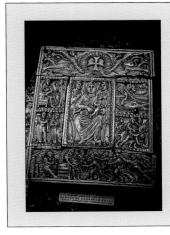

THE COVER OF THE ECHMIADZIN GOSPELS

The most outstanding Armenian carving in ivory is exhibited in the public showroom of the Matenadaran manuscript library in Yerevan—the ivory cover of the Echmiadzin Gospels. Older than the gospel manuscript itself, the ivory cover dates back to the sixth century A.D.

The cover of the Echmiadzin Gospels is fully comparable with the best examples of Byzantine ivory work, and has a series of panels showing the virgin and child, the flight into Egypt, the adoration of the Magi, the entry into Jerusalem and other episodes from the life of Christ. Both front and back plates show a pair of angels, bearing up a wreath in which is framed a cross.

SCULPTURE

Armenian sculptors have left their mark in stone, wood, ivory, and metal. The production of *khatchkars* or memorial stones by Armenians is unparalleled in the art world. *Khatchkars* attained artistic excellence in the 9th to 11th centuries, and are found in the hundreds in graveyards and near monasteries and cathedrals. They are rectangular, with the cross motif carved in relief in the central panel. The varieties are endless; hardly any are duplicates.

The most eminent stone sculptor of the modern period is Ervand Kochar, creator of the equestrian statue of the legendary hero David of Sassoun.

Armenian wood carvers have created column capitals (the top part of a column) and church doors, some of which are 1,000 years old.

Armenians are known as skillful artisans in silver and gold jewelry. The few earliest examples of Armenian metal work can be found in the museum at the rear of Echmiadzin Cathedral, in the State Historical Museum of Armenia, Republic Square, Yerevan, in the treasury of the Armenian patriarchate of Jerusalem, and in that of the catholicosate of Cilicia, now established at Antelias, close to Beirut.

Ervand Kochar, who is best known for his statue of David of Sassoun, is also a painter and a graphic artist.

PAINTING

Armenian art finds its most vivid expression in the illuminated manuscripts of the Middle Ages, produced around A.D. 600. When Christian texts were translated into Armenian, symbolic illustrations and introductory folios were added. The manuscripts were used in religious services.

Armenia's most renowned miniature painter was Toros Roslin, who worked at Hromkla and at Sis between 1260 and 1270. Hailed as the precursor of the Italian Renaissance, Roslin has an honored place in world art history. His works are kept in the Armenian patriarchate in Jerusalem.

The works of Martiros Saryan are exhibited in galleries around the world.

The Russian annexation of Armenia in 1828 saw a dramatic change in Armenian art. The most remarkable Armenian painter of this century was Hovhannes Aivazousky. A native of Theodosia in the Crimea, Aivazousky is described as one of the world's most thrilling and prolific masters of marine pictures. He gave his favorite works to the art gallery he founded in Theodosia.

The 20th century witnessed another dramatic change in Armenian art. The trend in Armenian painting became one of portraying optimism, joyfulness, and beauty, begun by the founder of contemporary Armenian painting, Martiros Saryan (1880–1972). Saryan's paintings became associated with Armenia itself—his landscapes, characters, and subjects became symbols of the country.

RUGS AND CARPETS

Armenian rugs and carpets are world renowned. The most common are the Kazakh and Karabakh rugs. These in turn can be classified into several well-defined categories, usually named after the individual villages and districts where they are made.

Well-known Kazakh carpets originate from Lambalo, Shulaveri, the Borchalo district, and Lori-Pambakh. Modern Kazakh rugs generally have large, bold designs and clear uniformity of color. They have a high pile. Kazakh rugs are usually heavy and dense, giving the feel of substantial body.

Armenian rugs and carpets go on sale at a weekend market in Yerevan.

Karabakh rugs are similar to Kazakh ones though the pile is often closer and the stitch finer. They show heavy Persian influence, being less stylized and geometrical than Kazakh rugs. Popular Karabakh rugs are the Lampa-Karabakh or Karadagh, which bear a resemblance to Persian rugs; Khan-Karabakh, which are mostly prayer rugs; Kazin-Ushag carpets, which have colorful plants and geometrical forms; and Channikh rugs, which often have a blue-black base color and fine stitching.

KOMITAS (1869–1935)

Komitas (Soghomon Soghomanian) was born at Kutina in Western Anatolia. He studied music and philosophy in Leipzig and Berlin before becoming a *vardapet* in the Armenian Church.

Komitas won global recognition as the renewer of Armenian national musical traditions. He collected more than 3,000 Armenian, Kurdish, Turkish, and Iranian folk songs and melodies. His original compositions, including choral works and compositions for orchestra and solo instruments, were published in a 12-volume edition.

Komitas' last public appearance in Western Europe was in 1914, in Paris, France, where he gave demonstrations of Armenian music at an international conference of musicologists. In 1915, he was arrested in Istanbul and tortured by the Ottomans. While he was spared the fate of many of his friends, upon his return to Constantinople he found his life's work—manuscripts, research findings on the *khaz* ("khahz") notation system (Armenian neumatic notation of the 11th century), and his library—in disarray. This plus his distress for the million and a half Armenians killed brought a nervous breakdown. Komitas ended his days at an asylum in Paris. His remains were repatriated to Soviet Armenia and lie in state in Yerevan, where his grave is a national shrine.

MUSIC

Armenia's long history in music can be traced in sculptures and architectural ornaments that show musicians playing various instruments and medieval manuscripts featuring figures playing pipes and flutes.

Armenia has produced several outstanding composers who have made their mark on the musical scene in Istanbul, St. Petersburg, and Tbilisi. Some renowned names are Tigran Chukhajian—who was called the "Armenian Verdi" for his masterpiece, the grand opera "Arshak II'—and Armen Tigranian, whose lyric drama "Anoush" is taken from the poem by Hovhannes Tumanian.

Armenia's contribution to the music scene lives on even today in the likes of sopranos Lucine Zakarian, Gohar Gasparian, and Lucine Amara.

LITERATURE

Armenian literature began to develop with the creation of the Armenian alphabet in A.D. 405 and the subsequent translation of the Bible. Moses of Khoren was the first to write in Armenian. His fifth century history of Armenia is the prime source of information concerning the epics, legends, and folklore of ancient Armenia and an indispensable reference on early Armenian history.

Through the centuries, hymns of religious inspiration were written by Armenians, including Gregory of Narek's *Book of Lamentations*, and St. Nerses Shnorhali's *Lamentations on the Fall of Edessa.*

Khatchatour Abovian was the first author to adopt a modern style. His novel, *The Wounds of Armenia*, tells of the people's suffering under foreign domination.

Among 19th century novelists, the best known is Raffi (Akop Melik-Akopian), the Armenian romanticist. His works evoke the grandeur of Armenia's past.

Opportunities for writers improved under Soviet Armenia. A well-known pioneer of Soviet Armenian literature is Eghishe Charentz. He wrote a number of poems about Lenin and was active in the creation of an Armenian Society of Proletarian Writers.

Opposite: **Armenian Aram Khatchaturian composes and conducts operatic and orchestral music.**

Below: **A memorial to Moses of Khoren, an Armenian historiographer.**

LEISURE

ARMENIANS ARE ACTIVE people who enjoy a wide range of sports. The competitive environment of excellence in international sports is prevalent in all sports in Armenia. Armenians are also avid soccer fans. Soccer games are held in large stadiums, back alleys, and yards in residential areas. The country's mountainous terrain presents a haven for avid mountain climbers. Armenians have also made a name for themselves in the international chess world, having produced many grandmasters.

SPORTS

In the 1996 Atlanta Olympics, the Armenian team proudly returned home with a gold and a silver in wrestling. The country was represented in 11 events at the Olympics, including free style and Greco-Roman wrestling, swimming, track, field, cycling, weight-lifting, boxing, tennis, and diving.

Armenians who have made their mark in sports at the international level were inspired by the same circumstances as other former Soviet athletes. They participated in many of the same events and trained under a united political climate. But Armenia's success at the 1996 Olympics confirms the Armenians' capability to perform independently in any field. Apart from the 60-member Olympic delegation sent by Armenia to the Atlanta Olympics, other ethnic Armenians not competing for Armenia include Andre Agassi (tennis, United States), Armen Baghdasarov (judo, Uzbekistan), Yurik Sarkisian (weight-lifting, Australia), and Andrei Sarafian (100 m kayaking, Kazakhstan).

Below: **Playing basketball in the school gym.**

Opposite: **Spending a hot summer day wading in the fountain in Yerevan's Republic Square.**

Armenian ninth world chess champion (1963–1969) Tigran Petrosian (left) makes a note to himself as opponent Mikhail Tal removes one of his pieces.

CHESS

In Armenia, as in other former Soviet republics, chess has become more than a leisure activity. For some, it's a living.

In the 18th and early 19th centuries, the French dominated the world of chess. But it was the Soviet Union that brought it to the world's attention, especially after the 1917 revolution. The Communist government hosted many important chess events and began a program of chess education for children, providing financial support for many of its best players. As a result, players from the former Soviet republics have long dominated the game. The only hiccup was when Bobby Fischer of the United States won the World Championship in 1972. Even though the Soviet Union ceased to exist in 1991, the world's finest chess players are still the ones trained under the Soviet system.

In Armenia, chess is practically the national sport, with both adults and children indulging. Children are educated in the finer points of chess at an early age. Many continue to pursue the game in more serious study. Chess as a form of education is highly encouraged. It is, therefore, not surprising that Armenia produces a plethora of chess champions and grandmasters.

Armenia's chess grandmasters are revered by Armenians and regarded as national treasures. The accolades presented to them include the naming of streets, schools, and chess palaces after them.

A famous chess palace is named after Tigran Petrosian, who placed the first stone at its foundation himself. He was the ninth world champion. His reign lasted for seven years, from 1963 to 1969. As a tribute to him, the Armenians erected his statue near the Chess Player's Palace and one of the main streets of Yerevan has been named after him.

In an effort to encourage young chess players in Armenia, schools, clubs, and societies have sprouted all over the country (especially in Yerevan) and have produced prodigies like Vladimir Kopian, three times world champion among juniors. Others include Elina Danielian, twice world champion among girls, and Levon Aronian, world champion in the junior boys group.

Armenia hosts many regional and international chess events.

THE GAME OF CHESS

Chess traces its history to India in the sixth century where it was called *chatarunga* ("chah-tah-ROONG-gah"), a Sanskrit word referring to the four divisions of the Indian army. *Chatarunga* later metamorphosed into the Arabic word *shatranj* ("shah-TRAHNJ"). The game eventually became known as "chess" when it was introduced to Europe by the Moors.

Chess is played on a board of alternating light and dark squares, which are referred to as white and black regardless of the actual colors. Each side consists of an army of eight pawns and eight other pieces—a king, a queen, two rooks, two bishops, and two knights. The game requires analytical skill in strategic moves and is won by reason and deduction. It is often referred to as a game of kinsmen, and is one of the few intellectually stimulating sports. A typical chess game can last for hours.

GARY KASPAROV

Perhaps the most famous of Armenian chess champions is Gary Kasparov. He was born to a Jewish father and an Armenian mother in the city of Baku in Azerbaijan in 1963. He was declared a chess champion at a young age and went on to become a chess master at the age of 16.

Eight years later, Kasparov won the World Chess Championship, when, at the age of 22, he defeated reigning champion Anatoly Karpov. At the time, he was declared the youngest player to hold the title in the history of the game. Kasparov has continued to successfully defend his title numerous times. He also serves the chess community by working in conjunction with the Professional Chess Association to transform chess into a household sport.

Kasparov speaks 15 languages, is an accomplished mathematician, and defeated the IBM computer Deep Blue in Philadelphia, which could determine a billion moves per second.

Kasparov is not a man of single interests. A tireless political activist, he founded the Democratic Party of Russia and actively participated in election campaigning. He is a vocal advocate for democratic reform in Eastern Europe and is renowned for his political and intellectual inclinations.

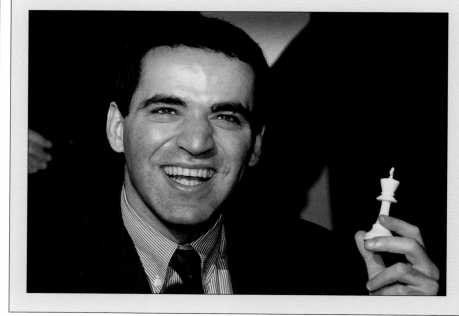

BACKGAMMON

A common pastime among Armenians is a slow, lazy game of backgammon which is played at almost any time of the day or night in just about any environment—be it in the comfort of one's home, the busy surroundings of a café, or in the shade of a tree.

Backgammon is probably the oldest game in recorded history. It is believed to have originated in Mesopotamia. Excavated relics and literary references indicate the game's popularity among the ancient aristocracies of Greece, Italy, Persia, and East Asia.

Backgammon requires two players, who move 15 counters on a specially marked board, according to throws of dice. The counters, black and white or in two other contrasting colors, are called stones or men. They are set out on a board divided into halves—called the inner and outer tables—by a partition, or bar. The tables are marked by 12 elongated triangles called points. The objective of the game is to be the first to move all 15 stones from point to point into one's own inner table, and then to continue moving them off the board.

Indulging in a friendly game of backgammon, a popular boardgame in Armenia. There are variations that allow any number to play the game, although only two people actually roll the dice and move the counters. The other players offer advice.

FESTIVALS

AS ARMENIA'S POPULATION is predominantly Christian, Armenian festivals, for example Easter and Christmas, are mostly associated with Christianity. However, these Christian festivals are celebrated in Armenia on different days from those generally accepted in some other parts of the world.

Apart from the traditional Christian festivals, Armenians also commemorate the Armenian genocide of 1915. Also remembered on this day are all Armenians who have been killed due to persecution or in the service of Armenia, such as those soldiers who died fighting for Armenian control over the disputed territory of Nagorno-Karabakh.

Armenians also celebrate worldwide holidays, such as New Year's Day and Mother's Day, both of which are public holidays.

Left: **Celebrating Independence Day, September 21, which marks the day in 1991 when Armenia officially broke away from the former Soviet Union and gained independence. Independence Day is celebrated with much fanfare all over Armenia, with the biggest attraction being the parade at Independence Square in Yerevan.**

Opposite: **Traditional dress from ancient times is worn for performances during Erebouni Yerevan, which celebrates the founding of the capital of Armenia.**

CHRISTMAS

The Armenian Church on January 6th celebrates the festival of Theophany as it was celebrated by the ancient churches. This is an all-encompassing celebration of the birth of Christ, the adoration of the Magi, Christ's baptism, and the revelations by the Jordan River. In later years the Syrian, Latin, and Greek churches changed the festival of Theophany into two distinct festivals: Christ's birth (Christmas) and baptism (Epiphany).

Most Christians celebrate Christmas, marking the birth of Jesus Christ, on December 25th. The actual date of Christ's birth has long been debated, with Gnostics and other so-called heretics choosing other days. The debate has since been divided between those who believe that it must be possible for researchers to uncover the real date of Christmas and those who think that the search for an exact date misses the point and the true spirit of Christmas.

The early Christians did not bother to celebrate the birthday of Jesus Christ because they expected him to return to Earth. Only after four centuries of waiting in hope for the Second Coming did the Church of Rome fix the date of Christmas as December 25th, replacing the pre-Christian festival of the Dies Invicti Solis (the winter solstice).

The selection of this date had a double significance: celebration of Christ's birthday and symbolizing the victory of Christianity over an earlier religion.

A choir boy all dressed up in his ecclesiastical Christmas finery, listening to mass.

THE FEAST OF THE ASSUMPTION OF MARY

The Feast of the Assumption of Mary is celebrated by all Armenians regardless of where they happen to be. Celebrated in August, the Feast of the Assumption has been tied to the ritual of the Blessing of the Grapes since early Armenian Christian times. The roots of this ritual can be traced to the ancient Jewish festival of the harvest of the first fruits.

Armenian tradition holds that about 15 years after the Resurrection of Christ, the Virgin Mary died in Jerusalem attended by all the apostles except Bartholomew (a founder of the Christian Church in Armenia). Mary was laid to rest by them in a funeral conducted with great piety.

For three days and nights, the apostles remained by Mary's tomb, where they could hear angelic choirs singing. When Bartholomew at last arrived at the place where she was buried, he pleaded with the other apostles to let him see her. When he had finally convinced them to agree, they opened the tomb and found that it was empty. The adherents of the Armenian Church believe that her body had been taken to heaven.

Armenians celebrate this day in church by singing special hymns written more than 1,000 years ago. Bunches of green grapes are blessed by the priest and distributed to churchgoers. Many take the blessed grapes home and share them with members of their extended family.

Novices leading the procession to pick grapes at the ritual of the blessing of the grapes to distribute to churchgoers. Many Armenians do not buy grapes during the summertime before this day. Celebrations often continue through the day with picnic gatherings.

Armenians in Fresno, California, have been celebrating this event annually since 1913. Each year at harvest time, Armenians gather to ask for the protection of the field workers and their crops.

Easter is said to derive from the pre-Christian spring festival of the Anglo-Saxon goddess Eostre, and many folk customs associated with Easter—such as Easter eggs —have a pre-Christian origin.

LENT

For Christians, Lent is a 40-day penitential period of prayer and fasting that precedes Easter. In the Western Church, observance of Lent begins six and a half weeks prior to Easter on Ash Wednesday (Sundays are not counted).

In the Eastern Church, Lent extends over seven weeks because both Saturdays and Sundays are excluded. Lent used to be a period of severe fasting: only one full meal a day was allowed, and meat, fish, eggs, and milk products were forbidden. Today, however, prayer and works of charity are emphasized. Lent has been observed since the fourth century.

EASTER

Easter is referred to as the "peak of all meals." This festival celebrates the resurrection of Jesus Christ. The spring festival has its roots in the Jewish Passover, which commemorates Israel's deliverance from the bondage of Egypt. For Christians everywhere Easter marks the crucifixion of Jesus during Passover (*c.* A.D. 30) and the proclamation of his resurrection three days later.

Early Christians observed Easter on the same day as Passover. In the second century, the Christian celebration was transferred to the Sunday, if the actual day fell on a weekday. Originally, the Christian Easter was one

The Catholicos of all Armenians at an Easter procession.

celebration. It was only in the fourth century that Good Friday became a separate commemoration of the death of Christ. Easter was thereafter devoted exclusively to the resurrection.

Easter is currently celebrated on the first Sunday after the full moon on or after March 21. The Eastern Orthodox churches follow the Julian rather than the Gregorian calendar, so their celebration usually falls several weeks after the Western Easter. In Armenia, however, Easter is celebrated on the same day as on the Western calendar.

In the Armenian Church, services on Easter Sunday begin at midnight with a procession. The priest and the congregation, holding lighted candles, leave the church by a side door and walk around to the main door of the church. The main door is closed to represent the sealed tomb of Christ. When the priest makes the sign of the cross with the crucifix he holds, the doors swing open and the congregation starts singing hymns. The church bells ring and the procession moves into the brightly lit church. Then the Easter mass and communion are celebrated.

ANCIENT CALENDARS

The earliest complete calendars were probably based on lunar observations. The moon's phases occur over an easily observed interval, the month; religious authorities declared a month to have begun when they first saw the new crescent moon.

During cloudy weather, when it was impossible to see the moon, the beginning of the month was determined by calculation. The interval from new moon to new moon, called a synodic month, is about 29.53 days. Hence, calendar months contained either 29 or 30 days. Twelve lunar months (354.36 days) form a lunar year.

To keep in step with the sun, lunar-solar calendars were formed by adding an additional month when the observation of crops made it necessary. Hundreds of such calendars, with variations, were formed at various times in such different areas as Mesopotamia, Greece, Rome, India, and China. The month was not always based on the phases of the moon; the Mayan calendar divided the year into 18 20-day months, with a five-day period left over at the end.

YEAR

In ancient calendars, years were generally numbered according to the year of a ruler's reign. Around A.D. 525, a monk named Dionysius Exiguus suggested that years be counted from the birth of Christ, which was designated A.D. 1 (anno Domini, meaning "the year of the Lord").

This proposal came to be adopted throughout Christendom during the next 500 years. The year before A.D. 1 is designated 1 B.C. (before Christ). Dionysius had referred the year of Christ's birth to other eras. Modern chronology, however, places the event at about 4 B.C. The first century of the Christian Era began in A.D. 1, the second in A.D. 101; the 21st will begin in 2001.

THE JULIAN CALENDAR

Romans, during the late republic, used various lunar-solar calendars. These calendars were supposedly based on observation, but were influenced by political considerations. The Roman calendar was in error by several months during the reign of Julius Caesar, who recognized the need for a stable, predictable calendar and formed one with the help of an astronomer, Sosigenes. The year 46 B.C. was given 445 days, to compensate for past errors, and every common year thereafter was to have 365 days. Every fourth year, starting with 45 B.C., was to be designated a leap year of 366 days, during which February, which commonly had 28 days, was extended by one day. This was not correctly applied, but was corrected by Augustus Caesar by A.D. 8.

GREGORIAN CALENDAR

The Julian leap-year rule created three leap years too many in every 385 years, and equinoxes and solstices drifted away from their assigned calendar dates. As the spring equinox determines Easter, the Church was concerned, and Pope Gregory XIII, with the help of astronomer Christopher Clavius (1537–1612), introduced what is now called the Gregorian calendar. Thursday, October 4, 1582 (Julian), was followed by Friday, October 15, 1582 (Gregorian).

In the Gregorian calendar, leap years occur in years divisible by 4, except years ending in 00, which must be divisible by 400. 1984 and 2000 are leap years, but 1800 and 1900 are not.

The Gregorian calendar is calculated without reference to the moon. However, the Gregorian calendar also includes rules for determining the date of Easter and other religious holidays, which are based on both the sun and the moon. The Gregorian calendar was adopted by Roman Catholic countries and, eventually, by every Western country and Japan, Egypt, and China.

YEAR BEGINNING

The Roman year began in March; December, whose name is derived from the Latin word for "ten," was the 10th month. In 153 B.C., Roman consuls began taking office on January 1, which became the beginning of the year. The Julian and Gregorian calendars retained this practice.

THE ORTHODOX CHRISTIAN CALENDAR

Up to the end of World War I, all Orthodox churches used the Julian calendar. In 1923, an Inter-Orthodox Congress held in Constantinople (modern Istanbul) introduced revisions to the Julian calendar so that it corresponded to the Gregorian calendar. This "New Style" or revised Julian calendar was adopted by some Orthodox churches, while others retained the "Old Style" Julian calendar. The Armenian Church bases its year on the New Style calendar. (Pictured is an Armenian selling a church calendar.)

EREBOUNI YEREVAN

Of lesser importance than the Christian festivals but celebrated with just as much zest is the festival of Erebouni Yerevan or the birthday of the capital city, Yerevan.

Erebouni Yerevan is an exciting and colorful festival which commemorates the city's birth almost 3,000 years ago and its developments over the years. The festival is usually celebrated on the first Sunday of October.

Yerevan was founded in 782 B.C. by the Urartian King Argishti I. The ancient name of the city was Erebouni. The festival started at the Erebouni Square where the remains of the old city are still well preserved. The events of Yerevan's long history are realistically recreated through theatrical performances and lively Armenian dances. The celebrations take place all day and everyone in the city participates enthusiastically.

PEACE DAY

While a Soviet republic, Armenia used to celebrate Peace Day. Peace Day, May 9, to commemorate the victory of the Soviet army over the forces of Nazi Germany, was celebrated all over the former Soviet republics. Peace Day was observed with a public holiday and parades honoring the soldiers who died during World War II. However, since the breakup of the Soviet Union, Armenia no longer celebrates Peace Day.

INDEPENDENCE DAY

Observed with a public holiday and parades, Independence Day, September 21, commemorates Armenia's independence from the former Soviet Union.

MARTYRS' DAY

A bleak day in Armenian history is marked by the Armenian genocide of 1915 when one and a half million Armenians were killed in Turkey.

In Armenia, massive throngs of people usually gather at the capital, Yerevan, march through the city, and lay flowers at an eternal flame to the victims of the genocide. The Tsitsernakaberd Park is a monument in Yerevan which was built in remembrance of the victims of the genocide. All government and church officials gather at the monument on that day.

Also remembered on this day are Armenians who died in the late 19th century at the hands of the Turks, and Armenian soldiers who lost their lives in the service of their country.

The Martyrs' Day remembrance ceremony at the Genocide Memorial in Yerevan is attended by President Levon Ter-Petrossian and officiated by the Catholicos of all Armenians.

FOOD

ARMENIAN CUISINE IS highly refined and varied. The original nucleus of local recipes has been greatly enriched over the centuries as Armenians moved from one place to another. It is impossible to say whether the dishes were originated by the Armenians and then spread to neighboring countries during their many migrations or if the cuisine was shaped by an incredible mixture of foreign influences.

Spices play an important role in Armenian cooking. Walking into an Armenian marketplace, one notices at once the smell of a variety of spices. There is the tart, pungent fragrance of crushed barberry, the cool sweetness of dried mint, and the unmistakable fragrance of fresh basil—all of which create an unforgettable experience, especially for the cook at heart.

Left: **A popular weekend morning activity is buying fresh fruit and vegetables at a farmers' market.**

Opposite: **An extended family sits around the remains of an enjoyable outdoor feast.**

A VARIED CUISINE

Armenian cuisine offers a wide variety of dishes with meat and vegetarian plates. Armenians are fond of stuffed vegetables called *tolmas* ("TOLL-mahs"). They stuff almost any vegetable—tomatoes, eggplants, zucchini, bell peppers, cabbage leaves, grape leaves, pumpkin, squash, quince, and apples. This passion for stuffed vegetables reaches its apex in a dish of assorted stuffed eggplants, bell peppers, tomatoes, and cabbage leaves called *Echmiadzin tolma.*

As fasting by abstaining from eating meat is a very important requirement of the Armenian Church, Armenians came up with many vegetarian recipes. One of the most popular is *pasus* ("pah-SOOS") *tolma* (meaning fasting *tolmas*), which consists of cabbage or grape leaves stuffed with ingredients such as beans, chickpeas, lentils, rice, potatoes, and herbs.

Feasting on roasted mutton and bread, washed down with bottles of wine.

Guests at an Armenian meal should be prepared for a feast that lasts several hours. Among the *meza* ("MEH-zah"), or appetizers, will likely be spicy dried meats called *basturma* ("BAHS-toor-mah"), *tolmas*, tasty meatballs with raisins and pine nuts, and home-cured olives.

Other popular dishes are *plaki*("PLAH-kee"), a vegetable or fish stew with tomatoes, onions, and olive oil; fluffy pastries called *bourek* ("boo-

These yogurt sellers do not have to worry about selling their product— yogurt in the form of yogurt-based soups or dips are present at every Armenian meal.

RAKE"), filled with meat, cheese, or spinach; spicy sausages called *sudjuk* ("soo-JOOK"); and pieces of meat on skewers, cooked over a charcoal fire, called *kebobs*. Armenians often sip *raki* ("rah-kee"), an anise-flavored drink, or one of the fine cognacs or wines produced in Armenia. Armenian cuisine also includes a wide selection of soups and stews. These range from richly flavored vegetarian and meat soups to simple vegetable and yogurt soups. Yogurt is found at every Armenian meal. In the summer it is served in the form of a cold yogurt-based soup. At other times of the year, *jajik*, a very popular yogurt and cucumber dip, accompanies practically every dish.

Armenian meals traditionally end with servings of fresh fruit and Armenian coffee, which is brewed in a traditional long-handled brass pot similar to those used in Turkey and the Arab states.

CHEESE

Cheese, called *panir* ("pah-NEER"), is a popular ingredient in Armenian cooking. Armenia produces several types of cheese, the most popular of which is a white cheese called *brindza* ("BRIN-zah"), made from sheep's milk. The Armenians often eat cheese either on its own or wrapped in the Armenian flat bread, *lavash* ("LAH-vosh"), sprinkled with herbs, green onions, and tomatoes. At typical Armenian meals, it is traditional practice to have cheese served together with assorted pickles, called *ttu* ("tetoo") or *tushi* ("too-she").

HOW CHEESE IS MADE

Cheese making is an ancient craft. By today's standards of industrial technology, the process of cheese making is still complicated, and combines both art and science.

Milk from different mammals results in variations in the quality of cheese. For example, milk containing high total solids (such as milk from sheep) increases cheese yields while milk high in fat produces softer cheese. The cheese-making process has to be modified in relation to the type of milk used.

Cheese-making capitalizes on the curdling of milk. The milk is carefully selected to make sure there are no harmful agents that could affect the process. It is heated and held at a specific temperature for a short period to destroy any harmful bacteria. Special starter cultures added to the warm milk change a small amount of the milk sugar into lactic acid. This acidifies the milk and prepares it for the next stage. Rennet (an enzyme from the stomach of a milk-fed calf) is added to the milk, and within a short time curd is produced. The curd is cut into small cubes and heated to start a shrinking process that changes it into small rice-sized grains.

At a carefully chosen point the curd grains are allowed to fall to the bottom of the cheese vat. The leftover liquid consisting of water, milk sugar, and whey is drained off and the curd grains allowed to mat together to form large slabs of cheese. The slabs are milled, and salt is added to provide flavor and help preserve the cheese. Later, it is pressed and packed into different-sized containers for maturing.

COFFEE

Coffee is traditionally served in a *jezveh* ("JAYS-veh"), a small copper or brass coffeepot. The pot is almost figure-like in shape, wide at the top, tapering in the middle, and wide again at the bottom. A good-sized spout makes pouring out easy. It has a long handle and no lid. *Jezveh* are also available in enamelware and come in various sizes, from a single-cup size to larger ones for six cups.

A traditional Armenian coffee recipe requires water to be brought to a boil in either a *jezveh* or a saucepan. The heat is then reduced, and coffee and sugar added. After the coffee and sugar have dissolved, the liquid is stirred for a few minutes until a thick black foam begins to rise. When this happens, the saucepan or *jezveh* is removed from heat and the foam is spooned into each cup before the coffee is poured.

Another popular Armenian bread is pideh, *a crusty loaf.* Pideh *can be baked in conventional ovens and are often brushed with milk or sesame seeds before baking.*

BREAD

Lavash or Armenian flat bread is traditionally served during all meals. A round, thin, crisp bread, it is sometimes called Armenian cracker bread. It comes in a soft version as well, and can be found in various sizes, ranging from 6 to 14 inches (15–36 cm) in diameter.

The bread is baked in a *tonir* ("toe-NEER"), which is a large hole dug in the ground with burning charcoal placed at the bottom. This hole serves as an oven for the bread. To bake the bread, the cook slaps flat pieces of dough on the already heated inner sides of the *tonir*. Once the bread is baked, it falls to the bottom of the oven and is retrieved with a pair of tongs.

Lavash is often used to make the *aram* sandwich. To make the sandwich, a softened *lavash* is spread with cream cheese, then layered with sandwich fillings such as meat, cheese, lettuce, and pickles. The *lavash* is then rolled jelly-roll style, wrapped in plastic wrap, and refrigerated for several hours. Before being served, the roll is cut into inch-thick slices.

TOASTS

It is traditional for Armenians to propose a toast at special occasions. The toasts are proposed at the beginning of the meal when all guests and key parties are present. The host then selects a *tamada* ("TAH-mah-dah"), a person who will lead the party and propose all the toasts during the event.

Armenian toasts differ from those of other cultures in that the *tamada* proposes an individual toast to each person present unless it is a big event such as a wedding, in which case the toasts are proposed only to the key people such as the bride and groom and their immediate families.

Toasts are offered as a sign of respect to the people present. A traditional toast offers praise, highlighting a person's strengths and good traits. The last toast of the occasion is always given to the host and his or her family, as an expression of gratitude. It is often said the best way to find out what others think of you is to attend an Armenian dinner and await the toast!

ECHMIADZIN TOLMA
(STUFFED ASSORTED VEGETABLES)

1 large cabbage, white, about 2 pounds (1 kg)
6 medium-sized green peppers
6 medium-sized tomatoes
6 long eggplants

To finish

4 cups boiling water (enough to cover the
    layers of stuffed vegetables)
4 tablespoons tomato paste

Stuffing

1 lb (500 g) finely ground lamb
1 lb (500 g) finely ground beef
1 medium-sized onion, finely chopped
2 tablespoons softened butter
$\frac{1}{2}$ cup short grain rice
$\frac{1}{2}$ cup finely chopped parsley
$\frac{1}{2}$ cup finely chopped coriander
2 tablespoons finely chopped fresh basil or
    1 tablespoon dry basil
1 tablespoon oregano
$\frac{1}{4}$ cup tomato paste
seasoning: salt, black pepper, chilli pepper

1. Discard damaged outer leaves of cabbage. Cut out the hard white core. Place cabbage in a large pot with lightly salted boiling water to almost cover it. Boil for seven to eight minutes. Set aside to drain and cool. Remove leaves one at a time.

2. Cut the tops from the peppers. Remove the core, seeds, and white membrane. Cut off the tops of tomatoes. Scoop out the tomato pulp with a spoon and keep aside the pulp. Halve the eggplants. Peel eggplant lengthwise, leaving strips of skin on it for a striped effect. Scoop out the flesh, leaving a quarter inch of flesh at the bottom and sides to resemble a small cup.

3. Blend the stuffing ingredients thoroughly.

4. Place a cabbage leaf on a flat working surface. Place a spoonful of filling near the bottom edge of each leaf and roll, tucking in sides to contain filling and to give the roll a neat sausage shape. Layer the bottom of the cooking pot with the excess cabbage leaves. Pack finished rolls flap side down in the pot. You should have two layers of stuffed cabbage rolls.

5. Place stuffing in vegetables starting with eggplants—do not fill them to the brim but leave space for expansion.

6. Place pulp from tomatoes over the last layer of cabbage rolls. Arrange stuffed eggplants and peppers over the rolls, and the stuffed tomatoes on top.

7. Mix tomato paste in a bowl with boiling water. Stir thoroughly and pour over the vegetables. Cover the pot, place on medium heat and bring to a boil. Reduce heat to low and simmer gently for 90 minutes or until the rice is soft.

8. Arrange vegetables in a serving dish and serve while warm.

A FOOD-LOVING PEOPLE

Food plays an important part in the social life of Armenians. They enjoy getting together over a meal. Armenians often invite friends, family, co-workers, or visitors from other countries home for a meal, where the guests partake of delicious food and savor Armenia's excellent wine.

Many of Armenia's festivals also center around food—such as the Blessing of the Grapes in the Feast of the Assumption of Mary—or are celebrated with a picnic or family dinner, such as Mother's Day.

Above: **This mother and daughter supplement their income by selling home-baked bread.**

Left: **Teaching a home economics class the rudiments of cake-making.**

ARMENIA

GEORGIA

AZERBAIJAN

TURKEY

IRAN

N

Alaverdi

Debet

Kura

Gyumri

Vanadzor

Dilizhan

Artik

Sevan

Aragats
(13,418 ft / 4,090 m)

Hrazdan

Lake Sevan

Razdan

Kamo

Echmiadzin

YEREVAN

Martuni

Armavir

Araks

**NAGORNO-
KARABAKH**

Ararat

Yekhegnadzer

Arpa

Vorotan

Goris

**NAKHICHEVAN
(AZERBAIJAN)**

Kafan

Kadzharan

Araks

●	Capital city
●	Major town
▲	Mountain peak

Feet	Meters
16,500	5,000
9,900	3,000
6,600	2,000
3,300	1,000
1,650	500
660	200
0	0

0 10 20 30 40 50 60 Miles
0   20   40   60   80 Kilometers

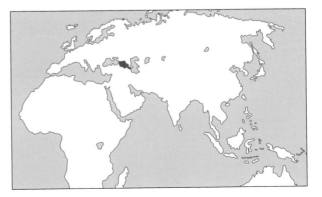

QUICK NOTES

OFFICIAL NAME
Hayastani Hanrape-tut'yun (Republic of Armenia)

LAND AREA
11,506 square miles (29,800 square km)

MAJOR RIVERS
Araks, Razdan, Arpa, Vorotan, Debet

LARGEST BODY OF WATER
Lake Sevan

HIGHEST POINT
Mt. Aragats (13,418 ft/4,090 m)

POPULATION
3.7 million

ETHNIC COMPOSITION
96% Armenians, 4% minorities (Kurds, Russians, Yezidis, Jews)

CAPITAL
Yerevan

LARGEST CITIES
Gyumri, Vanadzor, Echmiadzin

HEAD OF STATE
Levon Ter-Petrossian (b. 1945)
president (1991–)

NATIONAL HOLIDAYS
April 24—Martyrs' Day
May 28—Restoration of Armenian Statehood
   Day
September 21—Independence Day

CURRENCY
440 Armenian Drams = US$1

NATIONAL RELIGION
Armenian Apostolic Church

MINORITY RELIGIONS
Russian Orthodox, Islam, Judaism, Zoroastrianism

NATIONAL LANGUAGE
Haieren (Armenian)

SOME IMPORTANT ARMENIANS
Khatchatour Abovian—novelist
Hovhannes Aivazousky (1817–1900)—
   painter
Victor Ambartsumian (1908–1996)—
   astrophysicist
Tigran Chukhajian—composer
Gary Kasparov (1963–)—world chess
   champion
Ervand Kochar (1899–1979)—sculptor
Komitas, born Soghomon Soghomanian
   (1869–1935)—musician, composer
Mesrop Mashtotz (361–440)—creator of the
   Armenian alphabet
Tigran Petrosian (1929–1984)—chess
   grandmaster
Raffi, born Akop Melik-Akopian (1835–
   1888)—novelist
Toros Roslin—miniature painter
Martiros Saryan (1880–1972)—painter
Armen Tigranian—composer
Rafael Vaganian—chess grandmaster

GLOSSARY

Catholicos of all Armenians
The spiritual leader of the Armenian Church.

Cilicia
Kingdom founded in 1080. Also known as Lesser Armenia. The region of the plateau surrounding the central Taurus Mountains and the plain between the Taurus and Armanus mountains.

Greater Armenia
Kingdom founded by Artaxias in 189 B.C., which comprised the region of northern Armenia.

humus
Nutrients in the soil deposited by decaying vegetable and animal matter. Soil rich in humus is very fertile.

jezveh ("JAYS-veh")
A small copper or brass vessel traditionally used to brew coffee. A *jezveh* is wide at the top, tapers in the middle, and flares out at the base. It has a spout, a long handle, and no lid.

khatchkar ("KAHCH-kahr")
Rectangular memorial stones with a cross motif carved in relief as the central panel.

lavash ("LAH-vosh")
Armenian flat bread, usually thin and crispy and ranging from 6 to 14 inches (15–36 cm) in diameter. *Lavash* also comes in a soft version.

marl
Fertile soil with mix of calcium and clay usually formed in marine environments.

meza ("MEH-zah")
Appetizers served at a feast. Popular *meza* include dried meats, stuffed vegetables and fruit, and meatballs.

Parsi ("PAHR-see")
Indian name for an adherent of Zoroastrianism who fled persecution in Iran and settled in India.

Russification
The abandonment of customs and other cultural institutions and the assimilation of Russian culture and way of life.

satrapies
Provinces within the Persian empire governed by satraps (governors).

Tanzimat ("TAHN-zee-MAHT")
Turkish word meaning reorganization. *Tanzimat* was the name given to the program of modernization and Westernization of administration undertaken by the Ottoman empire in the late 19th century.

tolma ("TOLL-mah")
Vegetable or fruit stuffed with assorted mixtures such as beans, rice, and potatoes.

tonir ("toe-NEER")
A large hole in the ground with burning charcoal at the bottom used as an oven to bake *lavash*.

vardapets ("VAHR-dah-pets")
People who are religiously educated but not ordained as priests or deacons.

BIBLIOGRAPHY

Armenia, Then and Now. Lerner Publications, Minneapolis, 1993.

Hoogasian-Villa, S. *One Hundred Armenian Tales.* Wayne State University Press, 1982.

Kherdin, David, and Nonny Hogragian. *The Golden Bracelet.* Little Brown and Co., 1996.

Marsden, Philip. *The Crossing Place: A Journey Among the Armenians.* Kodansha, 1995.

INDEX

INDEX

INDEX

PICTURE CREDITS